from SAVAGERY *to* CIVILIZATION

The Power of Greek Mythology

from SAVAGERY *to* CIVILIZATION

The Power of Greek Mythology

Vincent Hannity
Illustrations by Erin Ann Jensen

Copyright © 2018 by Vincent Hannity

All rights reserved. No portion of this book may be reproduced in any form or by any means, including electronic storage and retrieval systems, except by explicit prior written permission of the author/publisher. Brief passages excerpted for review and critical purposes are excepted.

Illustrations © by Erin Ann Jensen. No illustration may be reproduced in any form or by any means, including electronic storage and retrieval systems, except by explicit prior written permission of the artist.

Cover illustrations: King Oedipus and Pandora's Jar by Erin Ann Jensen.

Book design and typography by Meggan Laxalt Mackey.

Library of Congress Cataloging-in-Publication Data
Hannity, Vincent, 1944 —.
    From Savagery to Civilization: The Power of Greek Mythology.
    Summary: "An overview of classical mythology for neophyte and experienced readers — an excellent companion and guide to the primary texts."
    Includes bibliographic information and glossary of characters.
    ISBN 978-0-578-41616-8   1. Trojan War. 2. Achilles.
3. Agamemnon. 4. Hector. 5. Priam. 6. Heracles. 7. Dionysus. 8. Apollo. 9. Artemis. 10. Athena. 11. Aeschylus. 12. Sophocles. 13. Oedipus. 14. Orestes. 15. Antigone. 16. Homer. 17. Iliad. 18. Odyssey. 19. Hesiod. 20. Theogony. 21. Roman myth. 22. Greek myth. 23. Virgil. 24. Aeneid. 25. Dido. 26. Gaia. 27. Eros. 28. Tartarus. 29. Titans. 30. Cronus. 31. Ovid. 32. Zeus. 33. Olympian gods. 34. Hera. 35. Poseidon. 36. Aphrodite.

FIRST PRINTING
Hector Press, Boise, Idaho

DEDICATION

*On behalf of my daughters,
Catherine and Margaret Mary,
I dedicate this book to the memory of
their brother and my son, Tom, who died young.
He would have enjoyed reading this book.*

CONTENTS

Acknowledgments xi

Timeline: The Classical World xii

Introduction 1

I   Birth of the Universe 7

II   Olympian Gods and Goddesses 11

III   Humankind Creation Myths 33

IV   Greek Heroes and Heroic Quests 41

V   Background of the Trojan War Myth 53

VI   *The Iliad* by Homer 61

VII *The Odyssey* by Homer 77

VIII Symmetry of the Homeric Epics 89

IX   Myth of the House of Atreus 95
      The Oresteia by Aeschylus: *Agamemnon, Libation Bearers,*
      and *Eumenides*

X   Myth of the House of Oedipus 107
      Sophocles' Tragedies: *Oedipus the King, Oedipus at Colonus,* and *Antigone*

XI   Roman Foundation Myths 131

XII Romulus and Remus 135

XIII *The Aeneid* by Virgil 139

XIV *Metamorphoses* by Ovid 151

XV Final Reckoning 159

Bibliography 173

Glossary of Characters 175

Illustrations 191

About the Author 193

ACKNOWLEDGMENTS

I OWE A DEBT OF GRATITUDE TO SEVERAL PEOPLE WHO HELPED AND ENCOURAGED ME ALONG THE WAY.
Thanks to **Bob Bushnell**, poet, short story writer, essayist, master chef, former attorney and businessman, and in general, bon vivant. Bob first suggested that I write this book, proofed early drafts, and graciously shared his wisdom from start to finish.

Thanks to **Rick Ardinger**, editor of Limberlost Press, and director emeritus of the Idaho Humanities Council. His invaluable knowledge and experience helped me through the publishing process with little frustration.

Thanks to **Chuck Guilford**, poet, essayist, associate professor of English emeritus at Boise State University, and author of *Paradigm: Online Writing Assistant*. He reviewed the manuscript, offered helpful ideas on how to improve it, and generously shared his publishing experiences.

Thanks to **Rosemary Reinhardt**, director of the *Osher Lifelong Learning Institute* at Boise State University, and her capable staff. The genesis of this book can be traced back two years when Rosemary invited me to teach an Osher course about classical mythology.

Thanks to my friends in the **Great Books Club of Boise**. They have provided me with intellectual sustenance for going on 40 years. They insist that I read, and prepare to discuss, each selection of classic literature on our schedule, even when the charms of other activities beckon.

Thanks to **Meggan Laxalt Mackey**, principal at Studio M Publications & Design, for her creative suggestions and graphic design of this book. And thanks to **Erin Ann Jensen** for her illustrations.

And finally, a special thanks to my wife, **Janet**, who encouraged me with constant love and support throughout the completion of this task.

TIMELINE
THE CLASSICAL WORLD

HEROIC/MYTHICAL AGE

Beginning to 3000 BC	First chaos, then cosmos
3200 – 1050 BC	Greek Bronze Age
2600 – 1600 BC	Minoan civilization in Crete
1600 – 1100 BC	Mycenaean civilization in Greece
1194 – 1184 BC	Trojan War between Greeks and Trojans. Greeks won.
1100 – 800 BC	Greek Dark Age

HISTORICAL AGE

800 BC	Alphabet introduced in Greece
776 BC	Founding date of Olympic Games
753 BC	Founding of Rome
800 – 700 BC	Homer. The *Iliad* and *The Odyssey*
750 – 650 BC	Hesiod. *Theogony* and *Works and Days*
600 BC	Sappho. *Poetry*
509 – 31 BC	Age of the Roman Republic
500 – 400 BC	**Classical Age of Greek Civilization**
476 BC	Pindar. *Odes*
499 – 449 BC	Greco-Persian Wars between Greece and Persia. Greece, led by Athens and Sparta, won.
525 – 456 BC	Aeschylus. Seven extant plays, including *The Oresteia* trilogy
496 – 406 BC	Sophocles. Seven extant plays, including *Oedipus* plays

TIMELINE
THE CLASSICAL WORLD

HISTORICAL AGE, CONTINUED

480 – 406 BC	Euripides. 18 extant plays, including *Electra* plays
440 BC	Herodotus. *The Histories*
431 – 404 BC	Peloponnesian War between Sparta and Athens. Sparta won.
410 BC	Thucydides. *The History of the Peloponnesian War*
399 BC	Execution of Socrates
380 BC	Plato. *The Republic*
323 BC	Death of Alexander the Great
146 BC	Rome conquered Greece in Battle of Corinth
323 – 146 BC	**Hellenistic Age of Greece**
264 – 146 BC	Punic Wars between Rome and Carthage. Rome won.
100 BC – 100 AD	**Peak of Roman Civilization**
44 BC	Assassination of Julius Caesar on March 15
31 BC	Battle of Actium. End of Roman Republic.
31 BC – 476 AD	**Age of the Roman Empire**
32 BC	Livy. *The History of Rome*
19 BC	Virgil. *The Aeneid*
8 AD	Ovid. *Metamorphoses*
100 AD	Pseudo-Apollodorus. *The Library of Greek Mythology*
110 AD	Plutarch's *Lives*
476 AD	Fall of Rome

Note: Nearly all dates are approximate.

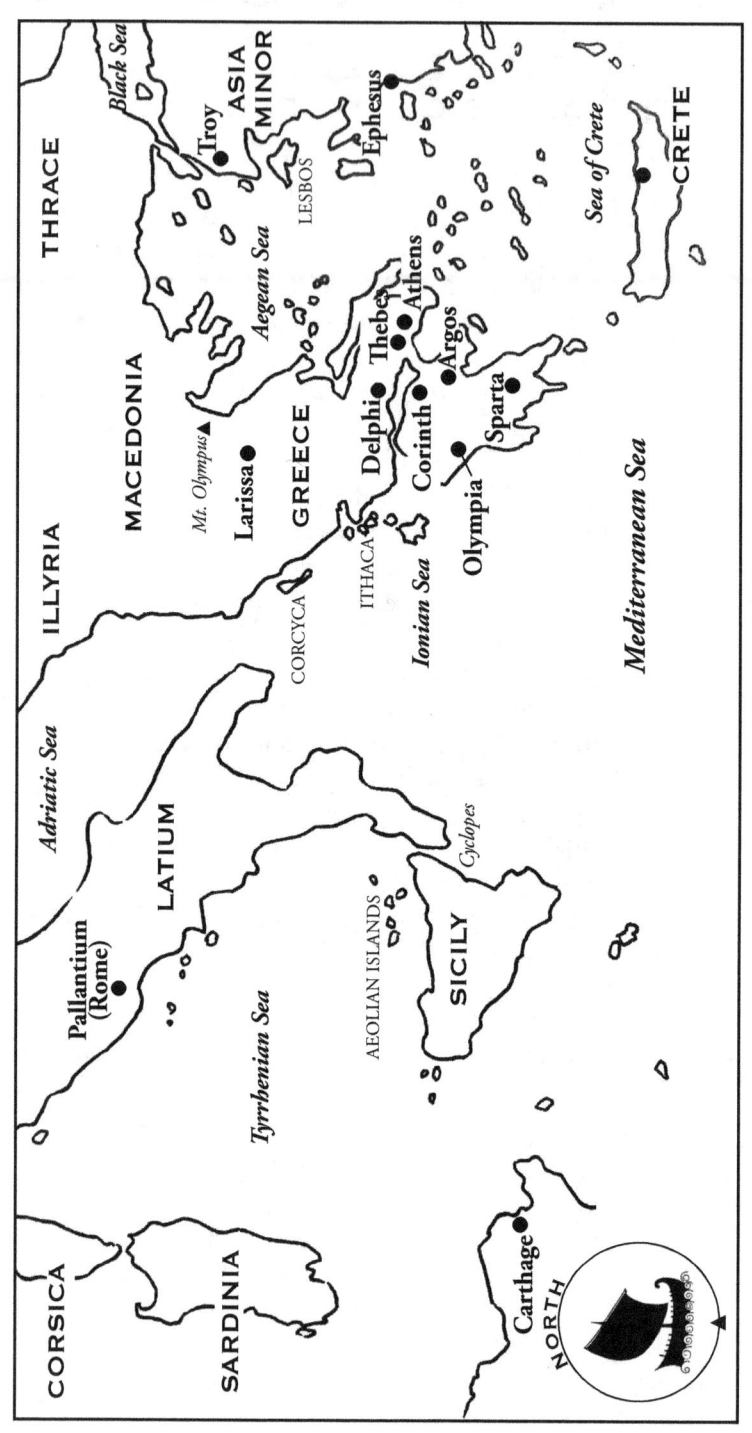

MAP OF ANCIENT GREECE AND ITALY
First Millenium, BC

INTRODUCTION

I AM A CLASSICAL LANGUAGES ENTHUSIAST. In the 50 odd years since college, when I last formally studied them, I have continued reading, discussing and sharing classical Greek and Latin literature with like-minded souls.

My never-waning enthusiasm stems from continually rediscovering the contemporary relevance of these works. Studying the ancients (Homer, Hesiod, the Greek tragedians, Virgil, et al.) is as meaningful today as it must have been in ancient times. (*Would you like to gain a deeper understanding of what it means to be human? The Greeks were among the first and best to seek that understanding.*)

By the end of this book, the overall flow of the ancient history resident in these myths should become apparent. And you, kind reader, can answer this question to your own satisfaction: *Why have the stories of classical mythology endured for 2500 years?*

WHAT YOU WILL DISCOVER

In these pages, you will read amazing tales:

- These myths are filled with massive amounts of blood and gore, tragic scenes of war, and individual revenge killings. Murder and mayhem reign throughout.

- Also, graphic sexuality, of all persuasions, by gods and men alike, permeate these stories. Something in these myths offends nearly everybody, so brace yourself.

- Along with sex and violence, you will witness the profound ability of mankind to withstand the severest forms of suffering, endure extreme physical and emotional pain, and still retain their humanity. Through suffering, man learned.

- You will see awe-inspiring heroism as Greek warriors face overwhelming odds for no other reason than to bring everlasting honor to their own names.

FROM SAVAGERY TO CIVILIZATION

- Often in the same stories, you will behold a woman of ship-launching beauty and goddesses of alluring sexuality.

- You may be moved by examples of genuine humanity — love, compassion, mercy. And finally,

- A renewed hope for mankind may surge in your breast, too, when you witness a weeping old man, clutching the knees of an enemy warrior, while the enemy warrior himself also weeps.

These are among the grandest stories of the Western cultural tradition, created in the embryonic years of that tradition during the Greek Bronze Age. They had an immeasurable impact on the lives of the ancient Greeks and Romans, and, as well, on the generations since.

MANY STORIES BECOME ONE STORY

These myths from ancient Greece, the characters that populated them, and the adventures that drove them, are strange and wildly diverse. So many myths, so many legends and fairy tales — conflated in dozens of towns and villages, intoned over hundreds of years, to people huddled around thousands of night fires. Their stories were ever changeable from place to place and time to time. No single document contains them — no Bible, Koran or Torah.

And yet, the aggregate of these myths relates just one story — the tale of how the ancient Greeks, from primeval mists, inched in fits and starts over thousands of years to reach the zenith of civilized society. It will be our task to discover how these many stories blossomed into a culture's one story.

WHAT IS CLASSICAL MYTHOLOGY?

The term *classical* refers to the two separate cultures of ancient Greece and Rome. The civilizations blossomed in different locations – one in Greece, the other Italy. Language separated them – the Greeks spoke Greek, Rome spoke Latin. And the two civilizations achieved their highest levels of accomplishment at sharply different points in history.

INTRODUCTION

Greek culture achieved much of its most memorable work in Athens in the fifth century BC, while Roman culture reached its apex of achievement several hundred years later, in the first centuries BC and AD.

Yet we consider the two separate cultures of classical mythology as a single unit. There existed between the two a strong relationship in their literature, art, and especially mythology. The Romans borrowed their mythology wholesale from ancient Greece and made it their own. As a result, we can discuss classical mythology as a unified whole and not just Greek mythology or Roman mythology.

WHAT IS A MYTH?

All societies create myths about themselves. It's unlikely that a society has ever existed without them. Myth is critical to a society's insiders. They are trying to understand their origins and create an institutional memory of themselves for succeeding generations. Myth is also critical to us as outsiders trying to understand a preliterate culture.

How can a culture that lacks writing pass down its values, traditions, and history? How can it transmit its view of the world, its beliefs about the gods, and the place of humans in the world? The only open means is traditional, word-of-mouth, repeated knowledge handed down from one generation to the next. That knowledge is almost always presented in the form of stories. So this is our definition of myth:

Myths are traditional stories a society tells itself. They represent that society's world view, beliefs, principles, rituals, and often fears.
Myths are stories told over and over again. They are handed down to those who follow. Once invented, myths are changeable and evolve over time. They grow with the telling – gradually and unpredictably. They usually recount events of the remote past, a time when things were very different in many ways.

From inside a culture, myths are viewed as being historically and factually true. They're presented as an accurate narrative of *what really happened* long ago and not very far away. However, it's rare for a culture to recognize its own mythology as mythology. Myth as a category really only exists when one is outside a culture looking in.

FROM SAVAGERY TO CIVILIZATION

MYTH OR RELIGION?

Myths often explain, justify, instruct, or warn. They may explain why things are as they are and how certain events or entities or conditions came into being. Examples:

- Myths may justify a certain rite or social institution, such as why and to whom sacrifices should be made at the end of the harvest season.

- They may instruct people in how they ought or ought not to behave. They may warn by showing the consequences of misbehavior.

Sometimes myth overlaps with religion and involves the gods. Religion refers to what people actually do to honor their gods – their rites, ceremonies, rituals and so forth. Myth refers to the underlying narratives that explain, justify, or go along with those rites, rituals and ceremonies.

Is a specific narrative myth or religion? The answer depends on whether or not the observer believes the narrative to be true. For example, from inside Christianity, the stories of the virgin birth of Christ and the resurrection of Christ are central all-important narratives. They're accepted as unquestionably true. From the point of view of a non-Christian, however, those stories are myths about the divinity of Jesus Christ.

MAJOR THEMES OF CLASSICAL MYTHOLOGY

As we trace the culture's progress from savagery to civilization, six major themes will continually seize our attention:

- **The will to power and the need to dominate** are inherent in the Greeks' creation myths. This drive for power sustained them in the relentless struggles of their most arduous times.

- **Fate – inescapable and unchangeable** – dominated the everyday lives of these people and their gods.

INTRODUCTION

- **The importance of taking responsibility for one's actions** in a world controlled by indifferent and apparently omnipotent gods.

- **The danger of *hubris*,** i.e., excessive pride.

- **The heroic code of honor,** which guided Greek behavior in all circumstances from their earliest days. And

- **The substitution of social justice and the rule of law over individual revenge justice**.

Let's begin at the beginning.

GAIA, MOTHER EARTH, primordial deity of the earth. A god or goddess could be both a natural force and an element of the universe. Thus Gaia was Mother Earth, in whose dust you could wiggle your toes. At the same time, she was a goddess who looked and behaved like a human.

CHAPTER I
BIRTH OF THE UNIVERSE

THE MOST COMPLETE SURVIVING GREEK ACCOUNT of the creation of the universe is Hesiod's *Theogony* or *genealogy of the gods*.

HESIOD'S THEOGONY

Hesiod composed the work in about 700 BC, roughly the same time that Homer composed the *Iliad* and *Odyssey*. Hesiod transcribed orally transmitted material. He did not make these myths up.

Hesiod's purpose in *Theogony* was to describe how the material universe and first gods came into being. He also described the birth of the later Olympian gods and the creation of humankind.

In the beginning, one primordial entity, Chaos (which means an empty void, not a state of disorder) existed. Somehow, Chaos gave birth to Gaia (the earth), Tartarus (the great region beneath the earth or the underworld), and Eros (sexual desire).

Eros is justified in being one of the four primary deities because almost all creation takes place through sexual reproduction. Eros appears later as a winged child, shooting arrows of love (Greek Eros, Roman Cupid).

Gaia first existed as a flat disc, like a DVD. She then shaped herself into the familiar earth of the Greeks. She placed the Mediterranean Sea in the center of the land, and produced the mountain ranges familiar to the ancients.

Gaia, without help, gave birth to Uranus, the sky. Imagine a transparent dome over the disc. Uranus then became Gaia's mate and equal, since he covers her on all sides. Below the disc was the underworld, Tartarus.

Gaia mated with Uranus. Together, this primordial couple, sky and earth, produced the first generation of gods, the titans, as well as the cyclops and other exotic creatures. The titans contributed important natural elements and entities to the landscape, such as the sun, the moon, and the River Oceanus, which continually flows around the perimeter of the earth.

FROM SAVAGERY TO CIVILIZATION

In this version of the creation, the primary forces generated their opposites. Thus vacancy created substance, darkness created light, and the earth created the sky. Further, these forces had sexes, and they copulated the way humans do. The female elements gave birth to yet newer forces.

DETHRONING OF URANUS

Uranus hated his children. As each child was about to be born, Uranus pushed it back into Gaia's womb. This caused Gaia great pain as well as great anger. In revenge, Gaia conspired with a younger male, her son Cronus, to overthrow Uranus.

Gaia produced a sickle. Cronus hid inside her body with the sickle. The next time Uranus came to have sex with Gaia, Cronus, from inside Gaia's womb, grasped hold of Uranus' genitals. He sliced them off with the sickle and threw them into the sea. They splashed when they hit the water, and from that splash was born Aphrodite, the goddess of love and sexual passion. From the blood that dripped from the castrated Uranus was formed the Furies, which bedeviled Orestes in Aeschylus' *Oresteia*.

At that point, Uranus, now neutered, retreated from Gaia. Thus, Gaia's children could emerge from her womb and thrive. Uranus became the dome of the sky. He never again took an active part in anything. He cannot be killed because he is a god, but he didn't go away either. (*You can go outside and take a look. The sky is always there. Check it out.*)

Under the rule of Cronus, Gaia's children, the titans, were free to mate with one another. They produced hundreds of children – water, trees, lakes, rivers and so forth. In this way, the titans' offspring completed the physical features of the earth.

DETHRONING OF CRONUS

Then erupted a second dramatic coup. Powerful Cronus learned that one of his children was fated to kill him. To prevent this fate from being carried out, Cronus ate each child his wife Rhea, a titan goddess, gave birth to, just as the child was being born.

As you might imagine, Rhea was visibly upset by this turn of events. So she hid her next baby and replaced it with a stone she had bundled up for Cronus to eat instead. Which he did. (*Cronus had never developed a taste for the finer things of life, so he didn't find the taste of stone off-putting.*) The saved infant would one day become Zeus, supreme ruler of the gods.

ASCENDANCY OF ZEUS

When he grew up, Zeus forced Cronus to vomit up all his brothers and sisters. The siblings then banded together with Zeus and made war against the titans. With the help of one sympathetic titan, Prometheus, Zeus and his siblings were victorious.

Zeus chained the titans to the bowels of the earth. They installed themselves as lords of the universe at the top of Mount Olympus. From that day forward, Zeus and his fellow gods were known as the Olympians, and Zeus was their supreme ruler.

ZEUS' DRIVE FOR POWER

The most notable feature of this creation myth is the drive for power and dominance from the very beginning. This is how Hesiod in his *Theogony* traced the gods – from savagery to, if not civilization, then to a peak of absolute control.

It wasn't so much that generations of the earliest gods succeeded prior generations. Rather, as the *Theogony* relates, each new generation of gods suppressed the prior one. Cronus suppressed his father, Uranus, by castrating him and rendering him powerless. Zeus suppressed his father, Cronus, by blasting him and the titans with lightning and shackling them forever in the underworld.

Thereafter, Zeus ruled on high – too strong for the law of retaliation that consumed his forebears. His was the invincible masculine will to power. He was the father who triumphed over Mother Earth and all other challengers. He was the strongest and therefore always right – the ultimate example of survival of the fittest.

Such was Zeus' reign in the third generation of his house. Power and dominance were the primary drivers. However, as harsh and brutal as they appear, the Olympian gods under Zeus were still the most enlightened generation thus far.

ZEUS, SUPREME RULER OF THE GODS — *the invincible masculine will to power. He was the ultimate example of might makes right. By necessity, the Greeks developed myths sufficiently powerful to sustain them in their harsh circumstances, explain their place of primacy on the planet, and propel them forward to a better world.*

CHAPTER II
OLYMPIAN GODS AND GODDESSES

THE OLYMPIAN GODS WERE THE PRINCIPAL DEITIES OF GREEK MYTHOLOGY. They consisted of an older generation – the siblings Zeus, Poseidon, Hera, Demeter, and Hestia. The younger Olympians were Zeus' sons Hermes, Hephaestus, Ares, Apollo, and Dionysus, along with Zeus' daughters Athena, Aphrodite, and Artemis.

NATURE OF THE GODS

The gods did not create the universe; they were part of it. They and the universe simply came into being. No external creator existed outside and beyond the universe itself.

Gods were anthropomorphic entities with volition, emotion, and bodily functions. They ate, drank, slept, mated, and felt emotions. They had bodies, but their bodies were much larger and much more beautiful than human bodies. They shared human emotions and passions, both good and bad.

A god or goddess could be both a natural force and an element of the universe. Thus Gaia was Mother Earth, in whose dust you could wiggle your toes. At the same time, she was a goddess who looked and behaved like a human.

The Olympian gods mirrored the kinds of creatures the Greeks themselves were, but on a grander scale. They were quarrelsome and unforgiving. They enjoyed warring, feasting, and fornicating. Their beautiful, powerful bodies and superior intellects reflected the highest of human ideals. And while humans had to die, the gods were immortal and could not die.

THE FATES: CLOTHO, LACHESIS, ATROPOS

With all these wondrous attributes, the gods, especially Zeus, might also appear to be omnipotent, but they were not. The gods were subject to overarching fate, or destiny, just as humans were. Fate is the inability of any mortal or immortal to change prescribed outcomes that stem from the Three Sisters:

- Clotho, who spins the thread of life;

- Lachesis, who assigns each person's destiny; and

- Atropos, who carries the scissors to snip the thread of life at its end.

Nothing can be done to alter or prolong one's destiny or a prescribed outcome. This was true of the gods as well as the lowliest mortals. Moreover, the Fates were independent of Zeus. They functioned separately. Even Zeus, generally speaking, could not counteract the workings of fate.

ZEUS, SUPREME RULER OF THE GODS

After overthrowing the titans, Zeus (Jupiter or Jove to the Romans) consolidated his power and became the supreme ruler of the gods. Sons would struggle no more to overthrow their fathers. No further shift of power down the generations. Zeus was the head god and would remain so for as long as the universe lasted. The whole story from the very beginning of creation led to Zeus' inevitable accession to power.

As ruler, Zeus gained physical control over the sky and earth. As part of his domain, he took control of the governance of abstract concepts that have to do with the orderly workings of human society.

- Zeus oversaw justice. He punished oath-breakers and validated the swearing of oaths.

- Zeus was the patron god of the guest-host relationship. He punished those who violated their duties to guest or host.

- Zeus oversaw prophecy. Apollo was also a god of prophecy, but Zeus was the main prophetic god.

Once Zeus had established himself as supreme ruler of the gods, he divided his power with his brothers. Zeus maintained dominion over earth and sky, but Poseidon controlled the seas, and Tartarus ruled the underworld. Zeus also oversaw the conceptual domains of his sisters (justice, wisdom, motherhood, et al.). He set himself up as the patron god of several aspects of human society.

PHILANDERING ZEUS

Zeus then began to mate with goddesses and human women, and to develop his reputation as an incurable philanderer. Philandering is not a behavior one expects from a god, certainly not the supreme god. But keep in mind that Zeus' sexual exploits had a purpose. They were not a matter of a god behaving badly.

Zeus slept around out of necessity and responsibility. It was his job to mate widely and freely – in order to populate his new domain. The Greeks could not abide polygamy, and so their supreme god — their chief *population increaser* — had to be promiscuous. And, by all accounts, Zeus tried his best to do a good job.

He certainly did get around. He mated with many, many human women. In the *Theogony*, one can easily find several examples of Zeus' mating with human women and the sometimes disastrous results that ensued.

He also mated with many, many goddesses, especially conceptual goddesses, such as wisdom and justice. Zeus was predominant in the Olympian pantheon largely because he was the father of seven of the major gods.

The sexual unions with anthropomorphic gods helped describe how Zeus populated his realm with critical concepts, and how they came into existence. Making him the father of justice, for example, underscored the idea that justice was part of his domain and part of human society.

And those pairings in turn resulted in yet other concepts. This became a way of talking about Zeus' attributes as a ruler. In addition, Zeus' promiscuity, as well as that of the other gods, helped assimilate local deities into the Greek religion, as the Greeks expanded their territories.

Overall, the myths about Zeus and the other Olympian gods and goddesses are primarily concerned with one thing: Establishing Zeus' mastery over gods and men.

FROM SAVAGERY TO CIVILIZATION

HERA, QUEEN OF THE GODS

Hera (Roman Juno) was Zeus' wife and sister. She protected marriage and childbirth. She was best known, however, for her jealousy and vindictiveness. Hera was the unaccepting wife of a philandering husband.

She jealously persecuted her husband's lovers and their offspring, including Semele and her son, the god Dionysus; Alcmene and her son, the hero Heracles; and several others. She was also angered at not being chosen the most beautiful of all the goddesses during the famed judgment of Paris. For this and other reasons, she became implacably angry at all Trojans. She especially despised Aeneas. She mercilessly harried him on his way to Italy to found Roman civilization.

POSEIDON, GOD OF THE SEA

Poseidon (Roman Neptune), a brother of Zeus, was lord of the sea. He was a wrathful god, easily angered and offended. He carried a trident – a three-pronged fishing spear that he used as a magic wand.

Poseidon was the primary divine opponent of the hero Odysseus during his journey home following the Trojan War. When Odysseus blinded the Cyclops Polyphemus, Poseidon's son, the blinded giant cursed Odysseus and asked his father to punish him. The angry Poseidon complied. He obstructed Odysseus' journey home at several points over the course of the epic.

DEMETER, PERSEPHONE, AND HADES

To the ancient Greeks, the changing of the seasons was a deeply perplexing condition. Fields mysteriously lie barren for a third of the year. Then a beautiful, flowery spring breaks out, followed by an eight-month growing season for crops. Why does this happen? The myth of Demeter and Persephone explained for the Greeks how the seasons came to change and why it was so important to them.

DEMETER, GODDESS OF GRAIN AND AGRICULTURE

Demeter (Roman Ceres) was the goddess of grain and agriculture and one of humankind's great friends. She first gave men the gift of wheat and taught them how to prepare it for food. People shared the seeds and knowledge of it with their neighbors, spreading agriculture throughout the inhabited world.

But Demeter was not always the happy goddess of summertime. She knew pain as well as joy. She was a suffering god and knew heart-rending grief.

PERSEPHONE, QUEEN OF THE UNDERWORLD

Demeter had a single daughter, Persephone (Roman Proserpina). One day, Hades, god of the underworld (Tartarus), decided he wanted a queen, so he left the underworld. He spied Persephone picking flowers in a field. He abducted her and took her down to Tartarus. Hades made Persephone his bride and queen of the underworld.

Demeter did not know what had become of her daughter. She wandered the earth in aimless despair looking for Persephone. Eventually, in her sadness and anger, Demeter forced Zeus' hand in order to get her daughter back. She caused a famine, and during the time of the famine, nothing grew on the earth. If the famine had continued, all humankind would have died.

Finally, Zeus sent Hermes (messenger god) down to Hades to set everything right. He struck a bargain between Hades and Demeter so that humanity would not starve to death.

HADES AND DEMETER SHARE PERSEPHONE

Under the agreement, Persephone would stay with Hades for one-third of the year and with Demeter for the other two-thirds. When Persephone returned to the underworld at the start of each winter, Demeter's renewed sorrow would render the earth barren. When Persephone returned each spring, Demeter's joy would cause springtime's blossoming and start the next growing season.

This abduction myth was primarily related to grain, which was important and rare in Greece. The return of Persephone from Hades was celebrated at the spring sowing. Hades represented the wealth of the grain that was stored in underground silos or ceramic jars during winter months.

FROM SAVAGERY TO CIVILIZATION

At the beginning of spring, when the seeds of the old crop were laid on the fields, Persephone would ascend and be reunited with her mother Demeter. At that time, the old crop and the new would conjoin in the fields. This union was the symbol of the eternity of human life that flows from one generation to the next.

GODDESSES NEVERMORE INNOCENT

The idea of sorrow was foremost in the story of Demeter and Persephone. Demeter was the divine sorrowing mother whose daughter dies each year. Persephone was the radiant maiden of the spring and summer time.

But throughout the season, Persephone knew that the abundant growth of the earth must wither with the coming of the cold, and that she herself will pass again under the power of death. She would never again be young and unequivocally happy.

Although Persephone did indeed rise from the dead every spring, she always brought with her the memory of the place of death from which she had come. Forever after, there was always something strange and awesome about her. She became the maiden whose name may not be spoken.

Most of the Olympians were happy gods, deathless gods, far removed from suffering mortals who were destined to die. But in their grief and at the hour of their death, **men could turn for compassion to Demeter, the goddess who continually sorrowed, and Persephone, the goddess who repeatedly died.**

DIONYSUS, GOD OF WINE

Dionysus (Roman Bacchus) is famously known as the god who gave man wine. However, he was also known as the raving god whose presence makes men mad. He incites them to savagery and even to lust for blood.

On the one hand, as Walter Otto tells us, Dionysus was the god of the most blessed ecstasy and the most enraptured love. On the other, he was the persecuted god, the suffering and dying god, and all whom he loved, all who embraced him, shared his tragic fate.

OLYMPIAN GODS AND GODDESSES
TWICE-BORN DIONYSUS

This duality within Dionysus became apparent in the myth of his birth. Dionysus was conceived by Zeus and a mortal woman, Semele. While Dionysus was still in Semele's womb, a torrent of lightning from Zeus destroyed her. The unborn Dionysus was in danger of perishing along with his mother. So Zeus took the child from the flames that engulfed his mother, and sewed him onto his thigh. Zeus cared for Dionysus until he developed and became strong enough to set forth in the world.

So Dionysus was a child of both the mortal and divine realms, born first from a mortal woman and then from an immortal god. He was referred to in the ancient world as the twice-born one, a god of dual nature and a paradox.

SUFFERING AND DYING GOD

The epithet, *suffering and dying god*, prefigured not only Dionysus' fate, but also the fate of those who cared for him. Tragedy or madness befell them all. In all the myths, Dionysus arrived in a violent and alarming manner. His presence awakened a sense of urgency, ecstasy, and terror in the hearts of everyone around him.

Dionysus literally possessed his followers and drove them mad. He made them do things that in their right minds they would never consider doing or even be able to do. This enigmatic spirit of duality and paradox set Dionysus apart from other gods. His was the spirit of a wild being.

The madness his arrival inspired was most clearly evident in the myths of the nymphs and maenads. Nymphs were minor female deities. Maenads were female followers of Dionysus.

These women took care of the young Dionysus. When he matured, his wild spirit possessed them and drove them into the mountains. There they nursed the young of wild animals, or else tore them to pieces and devoured their flesh raw. They handled snakes without suffering harm. They made milk, honey and wine flow out of the ground by beating it with a stick. They had both magical powers and extreme strength.

FROM SAVAGERY TO CIVILIZATION

The women welcomed the coming of Dionysus with insane behavior. The myth tells repeatedly how his fury ripped them loose from their peaceful domesticity and the humdrum orderly activities of their daily lives.

COUSIN PENTHIUS REFUSED TO BELIEVE

Perhaps because of the dual nature of his birth, other gods did not readily accept Dionysus as a god like themselves. In several stories, people resisted the worship of Dionysus.

In the play *The Bacchae* by Euripides, Dionysus arrives in Thebes to prove his divinity to Penthius, the king of Thebes and his own cousin. Penthius has refused to believe that Dionysus is a god and will not allow his subjects to worship him.

So Dionysus drives all the Theban women mad, including Penthius' own mother and aunts. He leads them to a mountain outside the city where they take part in his rituals. Penthius sneaks up a nearby tree, hoping perhaps to see some wild sex. The women discover him there. In their madness, they think Penthius is a mountain lion; they attack him and rip him apart. By the end of *The Bacchae*, Dionysus has proved his power and his divinity. Dionysus was a dangerous god to underestimate.

DELIGHTFUL DIONYSUS

However, the madness at the core of Dionysus' being was double-sided. Dionysus was certainly capable of the most appalling and dreadful acts. But he was also capable of the most life-enhancing and creative acts. The liberating spirit of Dionysus is embodied in his role as the god of wine, which had the power to arouse and inspire. It was said that in public festivals that paid homage to Dionysus, streams of wine spontaneously flowed. Grape vines blossomed and ripened in a single day. But, like all attributes of Dionysus, wine too had a dual nature: it could enchant, but excessive use could lead to inebriated ruin.

DYING AND RISING GOD

Another of Dionysus' many epithets is the *dying and rising god*. Because vineyards die in winter and return in spring, Dionysus was seen as a symbol of death and resurrection.

OLYMPIAN GODS AND GODDESSES

In a story about the birth of Dionysus, always jealous Hera convinces the titans to destroy him. The titans find him, catch him, and tear him to pieces. They eat all of his body except his heart, which Athena rescues. She presents the heart to Zeus. He turns it over to Dionysus' mother Semele, whom he had fetched from the underworld, to eat. Semele later gives birth to Dionysus again. The story represented the birth of the crops that die each winter and are reborn in the spring. Dionysus was the dying and rising god.

DIONYSUS, PATRON GOD OF THEATER

Dionysus was thus a natural to be the patron god of theater. Both tragedy and comedy were performed in Athens at festivals in honor of Dionysus. This god inspired behavior that was inconsistent with one's normal character. Actors acted out things they would not normally do. They wore masks. They acted as something they were not, and they created a reality that was not there before. Dionysus was the perfect god to supervise such an art form.

DIONYSIAN TRAGIC WORLDVIEW

At the core of this twice-born, paradoxical god was this ultimate duality – the Dionysian tragic worldview: **Everything always has its opposite within itself.** In the myths of Dionysus, madness, destruction, and death hovered over all those he touched. But so did the possibility for healing, redemption, liberation, and hope.

A final epithet expressed Dionysus' own duality/paradox — the *great ambivalent one*. He was the *divine archetype of all triumphant heroes and, simultaneously, the suffering and dying and rising god.*

ATHENA, GODDESS OF WISDOM AND JUST WAR

Zeus' first wife was Metis (Hera was wife number seven). Metis, a nymph who personified wisdom, was about to give birth. Zeus learned that she was fated to bear a daughter, Athena (Roman Minerva), who would be Zeus' equal in strength and counsel. But then Metis would bear a second child, a son, who would be a king of gods and men.

In order to prevent the birth of a son who would pose a severe threat to Zeus and ultimately supplant him, Zeus swallowed Metis.

He kept her in his belly, where she, as internalized wisdom, gave him counsel.

Nine months passed. Suddenly, Zeus felt a strong pain in his head and asked the gods' smith Hephaestus (Roman Vulcan) to comfort him. Hephaestus obeyed and opened Zeus' head with an ax without hurting him.

Suddenly, goddess Athena sprang from Zeus' head. Zeus, not Metis, gave birth to Athena from his head. She was already an adult, wearing armor with a shield in her hands and uttering warlike cries. It would now be impossible for Metis to give birth to a second child who would be a threat to Zeus, because she had not given birth to the first child. Plus, with Metis inside him, Zeus could add wisdom to his list of attributes.

Of the three virgin goddesses, Athena was the chief and was called the Maiden, *Parthenos*. Her temple is the Parthenon, which means *virgin*. (The other two virgin goddesses are Artemis and Hestia.) In time, Athena became the embodiment of wisdom, reason, and purity.

ATHENA THROUGHOUT MYTHOLOGY

In the *Iliad*, Athena was a fierce and ruthless battle goddess, who supported the Greek army. She represented the positive aspects of war such as its nobility, while Ares, the god of war, represented blood thirst and violence. The Greeks held Athena in much higher esteem than Ares, but later the Romans held Ares (now Mars) in higher esteem than all other gods.

In the *Odyssey*, Athena guided Odysseus on his 10-year journey home. As the goddess of noble or just war, Athena was closely connected to Odysseus because he had been a Greek hero in the Trojan War. As the goddess of wisdom, she was also connected to him because of his cleverness and intelligence.

Off the battlefield, Athena was warlike only when she defended the Athenian state from outside enemies. She was preeminently the Goddess of the City. She protected civilized life, handicrafts and agriculture; invented the bridle; and was the first to tame horses for men to use.

OLYMPIAN GODS AND GODDESSES

In the final scenes of Aeschylus' *Oresteia*, Athena oversaw the settlement between Orestes and the Fates in Athens, her namesake city. The settlement introduced the new law of social justice among men. She banished the curse of guilt from the House of Atreus as well as the obligation to assuage shame through revenge killings.

APHRODITE, GODDESS OF LOVE AND SEXUAL DESIRE

Aphrodite (Venus to the Romans) is usually called the goddess of love, but she was not. She was not a goddess of affection, or devotion, or lifelong companionship, or soulmate. She was, rather, the goddess of sexual desire or passion. (*A better epithet for Aphrodite might be goddess of the one-night stand.*)

We know from Hesiod's *Theogony* that Aphrodite was born in the foam that appeared around Uranus' severed genitals when Cronus tossed them into the sea. (*Aphros* is Greek for foam, so Aphrodite was *foam-risen* — also where we get the word *aphrodisiac*.) She was usually portrayed as a young woman who personified sexual desire and had reached the apex of sexual attractiveness.

As goddess of sexual desire, Aphrodite was extremely powerful. She could and did subdue even Zeus to her will. She could inflict sexual desire on Zeus. She could make him have affairs with mortal women, with other goddesses, indeed with whomever she wanted. The only beings she could not touch were the three virgin goddesses: Hestia, Artemis and Athena. But Aphrodite had power over the sexual impulses of every other living being – god, human and animal.

Aphrodite would often amuse herself by making gods and goddesses mate with mortals. The offspring of these unions were demigods or heroes. These were Greece's first heroes; their births marked the beginning of the Heroic Age.

ANCHISES' EXCELLENT ADVENTURE

Over time, Zeus grew weary and angry with Aphrodite for causing him and other gods to become sexually involved with humans and then boasting about her exploits. So he gave her a taste of her own medicine. Zeus caused Aphrodite to feel an irresistible longing for a particular mortal man, Anchises, a Trojan prince.

FROM SAVAGERY TO CIVILIZATION

At Zeus' direction, Aphrodite adopted the form of a young girl and seduced Anchises on Mount Ida, where he tended his herds. After they lay together, she revealed her true identity. Anchises was terrified and begged for mercy. Aphrodite hated the idea that she had mated with a mortal and would bear his child. She told him she would bear him a son, but forbade him from revealing to anyone that he had slept with the goddess Aphrodite. He did eventually tell (*couldn't help himself*), and was lamed as a result.

With her humiliation thus complete, Aphrodite stopped causing other gods and goddesses to have sex with mortals and producing mixed offspring. That's why the Heroic Age, which Aphrodite started, then came to an end.

The son of Aphrodite and Anchises was Aeneas, a famous Trojan warrior. After the fall of Troy, Aeneas led his people to Italy where he founded Roman civilization. Aeneas' complete story is related in Virgil's *Aeneid*. In it, Aphrodite, now the Roman goddess Venus, plays an important role.

SEX IN ANCIENT GREEK CULTURE

But let's return to Anchises' night with Aphrodite. Why did Anchises become terrified and beg for mercy, when he learned he had slept with a goddess? Because he knew that men who have sex with goddesses are always in big trouble.

As Elizabeth Vandiver tells us, it was acceptable in ancient Greek culture for gods and mortals to interbreed. Their offspring would be unusually exceptional human beings. Although sex with a god often had disastrous consequences for a woman, those were not inevitable. Some women mated with gods and lived normal lives afterward.

But Anchises knew that men who mate with goddesses commit a grave transgression. The reason why has to do with Greek views of sexuality and gender roles, and with the nature of the relationship between gods and humans.

The essence of sex in Greek culture was the domination of males over females. Greek culture was strongly patriarchal, and so the appropriate male-female relationship was one of female submissiveness.

When a god and a human had sex, the gender of each partner became very important. If a male god had sex with a mortal woman, there was no imbalance: a more powerful being (god, male) dominated a less powerful one (human, female).

However, when the male was human and the female a goddess, the relationship was unnatural and out of balance. A less powerful human dominated a more powerful goddess. Furthermore, sex between a god and human always resulted in a child. It was considered disgraceful and disgusting for a goddess to bear a human child. Thus, the unseemly nature of their relationship drove Anchises to beg for mercy from the goddess.

APHRODITE, PERSONIFICATION OF A NATURAL FORCE

Aphrodite was the personification of a natural force. To ask, *"Do you believe in Aphrodite?"* is an absurd question. Just as absurd as asking, *"Do you believe that sexual attraction exists?"*

It's also irrelevant to expect a personified natural force like Aphrodite to show compassion, mercy, or pity. The temptations Aphrodite caused and boasted about -- the improper sexual desire she created — devastated many innocent lives. But we should not expect her to feel compassion for her victims. The case was similar with Dionysus. The misuse of wine can destroy, but it's senseless to ask the wine to feel pity.

APOLLO: GOD OF THE SUN, PROPHECY, MODERATION AND REASON

The twins Apollo and Artemis were the children of Zeus and the goddess Leto. These two play crucial roles in our understanding of how the Greeks explained human experience and prescribed human behavior.

Apollo was known primarily as god of the sun, but he was much more than that. He was a god of youth, medicine, healing, music, prophecy, and, in general, moderation and reason. Apollo was represented in art as a younger man and the ideal of youthful, manly beauty.

Apollo was the patron of music and the arts. As such, he presided over nine goddesses, called the Muses. In early stages of Greek culture, the Muses were simply personifications of the creative arts in general. They did not yet have their own areas of expertise.

Not all of Apollo's images were positive. He was also associated with sudden death, as well as plague and death through disease. He was often shown wearing a quiver and carrying a bow. When he shot men with the arrows from his quiver, they fell dead.

APOLLO, GOD OF PROPHECY

Apollo's most important attribute was his prophetic gift. He was the god of prophecy, second only to Zeus.

The most important oracular shrine in Greece was at Delphi, which was sacred to Apollo. His role as a god was to provide prophecy for humans.

People traveled to Delphi to ask the priestess their questions about anything at all. They would give their questions to the priestess. She would declare an oracular answer given to her by Apollo. Many of the prophecies, or oracles, that the priestess gave were very ambiguous.

APOLLO'S ORACLE AT DELPHI

As we learn from Herodotus in his *Histories*, one of the most famous oracles was given to the king of Lydia, Croesus, in about 550 BC. He came to Delphi to ask Apollo if he should declare war on Persia, which was ruled by the Emperor Cyrus. Croesus asked, "*Should I attack Cyrus' kingdom?*"

Apollo, through the priestess, answered, "*If you cross the river Halys* (which was the boundary between their two empires), *you will destroy a great empire.*"

Croesus took this as a positive answer, went to war with Cyrus, and, of course, destroyed his own empire. The highly ambiguous oracle could have been read either way, and Croesus read it the wrong way. It was always difficult to tell what exactly the oracles meant.

Apollo's role as the patron of prophecy reflected his overall association with reason, moderation, and the notion that there was order in the world. The Greeks believed that Apollo somehow knew and foreknew this order, so he could foretell the future.

OLYMPIAN GODS AND GODDESSES

The oracle at Delphi was taken very seriously by the Greeks and their neighbors. Cities sent representatives to the oracle to ask for advice before they undertook anything important. For example, during the Persian Wars of 490 to 480 BC, Athens was besieged by the Persians. Several times, the Athenians asked Apollo's oracle at Delphi, "*What should we do? Should we evacuate our city,* or *should we stand and fight?*"

In response, the Athenians received several contradictory oracular answers. These responses, taken together, were ambiguous to such a degree that, in effect, they amounted to no answer at all.

MAXIMS CARVED AT DELPHI

Greek religion had no orthodoxy or single sacred text. Nor did it have prescriptive commandments, such as *thou shalt this* or *thou shalt not that*.

However, carved on Apollo's temple at Delphi were two phrases that came as close as Greek religion ever did to commandments. These two sayings were:

Know Yourself

Nothing in Excess

Know Yourself meant to remember what kind of creature you are. Remember your limitations. Remember, above all else, that you are not a god.

These two sayings encapsulated a theme that ran throughout Greek myth – the idea that humans were liable when they transgressed the boundaries that separated them from the gods. To do so inevitably brought suffering.

If you forgot what kind of a creature you are, or if you had anything in excess – especially an excess of good things or self-esteem – you were in danger of offending the gods. You would suffer the consequences.

NIOBE'S TEARS

In particular, humans must avoid *hubris* or excessive or overweening pride – the kind of excessive pride that leads a person to claim more than his or her due. It was very important to obey Apollo's maxims

Know Yourself and *Nothing in Excess*, and to avoid the dangers of *hubris*. The story of Niobe is a perfect example.

Niobe was the queen of Thebes. She boasted that she was more worthy of worship than the goddess Leto, the mother of Apollo and Artemis. She reasoned that Leto had only a paltry two children, whereas she, Niobe, had 14 children. The people of Thebes should build a temple to worship her, Niobe said, rather than one to Leto, because Niobe had seven times more children than Leto had.

This was a big mistake. Niobe clearly did not know herself. She forgot a crucial difference: her children were human; Leto's children, Apollo and Artemis, were gods.

Upon hearing this, Apollo and Artemis, both armed with bows and arrows, reacted. Apollo shot Niobe's seven young sons, who at that moment were out exercising. They fell dead at Niobe's feet. That was a tragic turn of events for Niobe for sure.

But did she learn her lesson? No. She said that she was still better off than Leto. She still had her seven daughters, and Leto still had just two children. At this point, Artemis began putting arrows to the bow and shooting Niobe's seven daughters. When only the youngest was left, Niobe begged for mercy. She asked Artemis to spare her youngest child. But it was too late – the arrow had already left the bow. Even the youngest, about two years old, died before her eyes.

So there was Niobe, surrounded by the corpses of her 14 children, who all died because of her *hubris*. Niobe herself was then transformed into a statue with water running down the face, forever symbolizing Niobe's tears for her children.

NIOBE'S TRANSGRESSIONS

This myth demonstrates how we should interpret these two maxims, *Know Yourself* and *Nothing in Excess*, and what happens when you fail to abide by them. The two maxims work together, almost as two sides of the same coin. Niobe failed to know herself. She failed to remember what it means to be human – that humans are, by definition, vulnerable to death.

The fact that she had 14 children today did not mean that she would have 14 children tomorrow. She may lose some of them; she may lose all of them. They are human; therefore, they can die at any moment. Human good fortune is changeable and unstable. It can disappear in the blink of an eye.

But why did Niobe fail to know herself? Why did she succumb to *hubris* and forget her human vulnerability to death? Because of excess. She had so many children, all of them alive, that she thought she was safe. If two or three died, she would still have 11 or 12. Even if half of them died, she would still have seven.

Niobe thought that, because of this large number of children, she was safe, and that she was not liable to normal human experience. That was her great error. Apollo, as a god of reason and moderation, warns us that we should have nothing in excess, because that is so dangerous. We should, all of us, practice moderation, or else.

ARTEMIS, GODDESS OF THE HUNT

Apollo's twin sister, Artemis (Roman Diana), was the Olympian goddess of hunting and wildness.

In some ways, Artemis was Apollo's polar opposite. She was a huntress, the patron of wild beasts, and the protector of the young of all species, especially young girls. As a huntress, she carried a bow and wore a quiver. She was often shown in a short robe that would allow for running. Artemis was associated with wildness and wild things, while Apollo was associated with reason and civilization. Artemis was linked with nature, Apollo with culture.

There was a dark side to Artemis. Like Apollo, Artemis could bring sudden death, as we saw in the story of Niobe. She could bring diseases to women or cleanse them of disease, whenever she wanted. Artemis became vengeful when crossed, especially when she witnessed the transgression of the boundaries between humans and gods.

ACTAEON'S TRANSGRESSION

Even an unintentional violation of those boundaries could lead to disaster for the human, as we see in the story of Actaeon. Actaeon was a great hunter. He was out in the woods one day, hunting with his friends and hunting dogs. He became separated from his companions. As he wandered through the woods, he came upon a lake. In the lake was Artemis bathing, nude.

Actaeon did not intend to see Artemis naked. It was unintentional, a mistake, he didn't mean to, it wasn't his fault. Too bad. His intentions didn't matter. Artemis became enraged and immediately punished Actaeon by transforming him into a stag. She left his mind perfectly aware of what was happening to him. He had an animal body, but a human mind.

As Actaeon, now a stag, ran through the woods, his own hounds picked up his scent. With his friends urging the hounds on, they chased Actaeon down, killed him, and tore him to shreds. His friends stood around wondering where Actaeon was -- he was missing out on all the fun.

ACTIONS ARE WHAT MATTER

This dreadful story tells us something important about the worldview represented in classical mythology. In this worldview, intentions are quite frequently irrelevant. **Actions are what matter. What mattered was not what Actaeon intended. What mattered was what Actaeon did.** He saw Artemis naked. He suffered the consequences. And, as was often the case, the punishment was extremely outsized relative to the unintended slight.

SACRIFICE OF IPHIGENIA

In another famous myth, Agamemnon, commander of the Greek armed forces on their way to fight the Trojan War, deeply offended Artemis. Agamemnon had killed her sacred deer and then praised himself as a better hunter than the goddess. To the goddess, this was a clear case of *hubris*. She retaliated by halting the winds and rendering the Greek ships motionless.

To atone for Agamemnon's foolish boasting, Artemis demanded that he sacrifice his own daughter, Iphigenia. And so Agamemnon did. He sacrificed his own daughter to satisfy Artemis, and she in turn restored favorable winds. It was such a terrible punishment for

OLYMPIAN GODS AND GODDESSES

such a minor infraction – the sacrifice of a young girl, like a sacrificial animal, to atone for the sin of an idle boast. For this act, Agamemnon would one day suffer mightily.

FROM MYSTERIOUS TO STEREOTYPICAL

The sources of these myths about the Olympian gods range from Hesiod to Ovid, a span of about 800 years. Yet there's a certain consistency about them. Most revolve around conflict. The Greeks were contentious and loved fights, contests, battles of wit, the Homeric epics, the Olympic Games, the dialogues of Plato, the drama festivals, and the public trials. The ancient Greeks were forever warring among themselves. It was their way of life, and it resulted in a dynamic though unstable civilization.

KEEN SENSE OF HONOR

The primary source of conflict among these myths of the gods was a keen sense of honor. The Greeks accepted diverse gods because the gods behaved in the diverse ways the Greeks themselves behaved. Gods and goddesses did possess a very sharp sense of what was owed to them. The Greeks were a proud people, and their gods and goddesses lived by pride. Handsome, vigorous, immortal – the deities were always exceedingly jealous of their own honor.

MINOR OFFENSES, MAJOR PUNISHMENTS

That in turn led to a common theme found in these myths: mortals who infringe upon the rights of the gods suffer terrible punishments. Indeed, sometimes the punishments are far more severe than the corresponding offenses seem to justify.

We've seen several examples:

- For accidentally seeing Artemis nude, Actaeon was transformed into a stag and killed by his own hunting dogs.

- Anchises slept with Aphrodite, talked about it, and was lamed.

- For refusing to believe that Dionysus was a god, Penthius was torn limb from limb by Dionysus' women followers.

- Agamemnon bragged that he was a better hunter than Artemis and was forced to sacrifice his own daughter Iphigenia to atone for his boast. And

- Niobe boasted of being better than the goddess Leto because Leto had fewer children, until Apollo and Artemis killed all 14 of Niobe's.

VEGETATION MYTHS

As James Weigel summarizes, two of the myths have been called vegetation myths. The story of Demeter was connected to the annual birth and death of grain. The myth of Dionysus was related to the cycle of the vine. Unlike other gods, both deities underwent great suffering – Demeter through the repeated loss of her daughter and Dionysus through his own dismemberment.

In each case, the underworld, the kingdom of death, played an important role. Every living thing must one day descend into the kingdom of death. But the myth taught the Greeks that Persephone and Dionysus were able to emerge from death, just as grains and grapes perennially emerge – thus holding out the hope of resurrection to mortal man.

The gods each had their own personality, depending on their function. Thus, it was natural for Poseidon to be tempestuous as the god of the sea, and for Artemis to be mannish as the goddess of the hunt, and for Aphrodite to be seductive as the goddess of sexual passion.

LOSS OF TRANSCENDENT QUALITY

Yet while the particulars of the nature of the gods became more vivid in the minds of man, the gods gradually lost their transcendent quality. Their aura of mystery became less mysterious. What was once dynamic about the gods gradually became static.

Once their characters, functions, and deeds were thoroughly understood, their natures could not develop any further. There was nowhere for them to go. For all their glamour, the gods became lifeless stereotypes, gradually losing their power to affect human lives. In the fullness of time, people ceased to believe in them.

ATHENA, goddess of wisdom and just war. Zeus, not her mother Metis, gave birth to Athena from his head. Thus, Metis' next birth could not be her second, which a prophecy said would be a Zeus-supplanting son. At birth, Athena, fully grown, wore armor with a shield in her hand and uttered warlike cries.

PROMETHEUS, man's best friend, created men to stand upright like the gods, gave men fire stolen from the gods, and taught men how to outwit the gods.

CHAPTER III
HUMANKIND CREATION MYTHS

So now the cosmos was in place. The war between the titans and the Olympians was over. And Zeus with his dozen or so Olympian gods and goddesses sat comfortably atop Mt. Olympus. It was time for humankind to enter the picture.

PROMETHEUS, MAN'S BEST FRIEND

According to Hesiod, two of the titans were spared imprisonment in Tartarus after the war – Prometheus and his brother Epimetheus. They were assigned the task of creating humans. Epimetheus bungled his part of the job of human creation. He gave animals all the really useful qualities – such as swiftness, cunning, strength, fur, or wings. That left no valuable attributes for man.

So Prometheus stepped in. He created man to stand upright, just like the gods. Then he gave man the most precious gift of all — fire, which he stole from the gods. He also showed man how to occasionally outwit the gods. For example, when men sacrificed animals to the gods, Prometheus tricked Zeus into accepting the worst parts of the animal, thus leaving the best parts for men.

Zeus was outraged at Prometheus for this double treachery. He punished Prometheus by chaining him to a rock in the Caucasus Mountains. Every day an eagle, Zeus' sacred bird, flew to the rock and ate Prometheus' liver. Every night, his liver would grow back again. *The next day, all would be quiet until someone would cry out, "The eagle has landed!" And then Prometheus would be "de-livered" one more time.* This was to go on forever.

THE WAY IT WAS

The mythical world of the gods was indeed harsh. But the world of humans was even harsher. In the case of the crimes of Prometheus, Zeus became just as angry with men as he was with Prometheus, even though men did no more than accept his help.

FROM SAVAGERY TO CIVILIZATION

But the gods' ruthless treatment of men accurately reflected the real bleakness of these people's lives. They ground out a subsistence existence, dominated by fate. A state of constant war often existed among individuals, families, and villages. And the gods continually harried them with onerous hardships. The Prometheus episode was only an early example.

PANDORA: THE FIRST WOMAN

So, unsurprisingly, Zeus meted out a horrible punishment for mankind – one just as awful as having one's liver eaten out every day. That awful punishment was to bring in... *women*. Zeus intended women to punish men and cause them eternal trouble.

The first woman, of course, was Pandora, which means *gift of all*. She indeed brought eternal suffering upon humanity – because of her curiosity. The gods gave Pandora a jar (the Greek word means *jar*, not box) and told her never to open it.

That jar contained all the evils that afflict humankind – diseases, old age, care, trouble – as well as hope. But as we know, Pandora foolishly opened the lid of the jar. All the evils of the universe flew out, except for hope, which remained inside just under the jar's lid. Thus raising the eternal question: *Why did hope stay in that jar?*

WHY HOPE STAYED IN PANDORA'S JAR

Elizabeth Vandiver describes two common but contradictory interpretations of why hope stayed in Pandora's jar.

According to one, the presence of hope in the jar indicated that, no matter how bad things would get, mankind still had hope. This interpretation ignores a couple of things:

- First, hope was still in the jar. It was not out in the world with the other evils. Its status was somehow different from the other things in the jar. No one has ever teased out what that somewhat different status might be.

- Second, if hope was a good thing, why was it in the jar of evils to begin with? What was it doing there? Again, no answers have ever come forth.

Another extreme interpretation is more pessimistic. It contends that hope's retention in the jar meant that there was no hope – even that tiny consolation for humankind was utterly absent. There was no hope; mankind might as well just lie down and die. That seems unduly pessimistic, even for the Greeks.

Vandiver offers an alternative explanation. The key may be that the word we translate as hope, *elpis* in Greek, is not an unambiguously good thing. It might be better translated as *expectation* rather than hope. An expectation can be good, but it can also be bad.

- If hope gets you through a dreadful situation, and things did come out right for you in the end, then hope is a good thing.

- On the other hand, if you go for years with a false expectation that something will happen that never does, and all your chances disappear, because that expectation was never fulfilled, then hope is an evil thing.

PANDORA'S JAR contained all the evils that afflict humankind – diseases, old age, care, trouble – as well as hope. When Pandora foolishly opened the lid of the jar, all the evils of the universe flew out, except for hope, which remained inside. Why did hope stay in that jar?

Thus, the ambiguous nature of hope may be the key point here – that hope can be both good and evil. This may explain why it was caught under the lid of the jar. Hope is not entirely good, so it was in the jar to begin with. And hope is not entirely evil, so it could not escape into the world.

PANDORA'S JAR AS PANDORA'S WOMB

The myth of Pandora lends itself to psychological interpretation. The jar was a womb-shaped object and can be read as representing Pandora's womb. (That's why it's a jar and not a box.)

Pandora and all women are responsible for evil in the sense that they are responsible for life itself. They give birth. They put new humans into the world to experience life, which means experiencing evil. Birth inflicts all the evils of life on the individual person who is born.

But, at the same time, birth is humankind's only source of new generations. It provides the only hope for the human race to continue. Birth, like hope in the jar, is ambiguous. It imposes evil on the individual but gives hope to the race.

ANXIETIES OF A PATRIARCHAL SOCIETY

On another level, the Pandora myth may represent the anxieties of a patriarchal society.

In a strongly patriarchal society, which ancient Greece was, it was all important for men to have sons. They required sons to carry on the family name, leave their property to, and so forth. The only way to achieve sons was through women.

Thus women controlled men's ultimate destiny. If the woman remained barren, the man remained barren. Man had children only if the woman provided them. Again, the jar – which, remember, Pandora chose to open but could have chosen to leave closed – the jar could represent this fear of women's power over reproduction.

Thus, the whole description of Pandora can be read as reflecting male anxieties about, and resentments of, sexual reproduction. This was a common theme in Greek literature. It was not uncommon for a male character (i.e., Jason in Euripides' play *Medea*) to say that mortals should reproduce in ways other than with women, and that the female sex should not even exist.

HUMANKIND CREATION MYTHS

RELATIONSHIP BETWEEN GODS AND HUMANS

Let's consider the ways gods and humans interacted with one another in Greek mythology.

- First, the gods did not love humans; they did not feel compelled to treat humans fairly. This was not a relationship of love, compassion or mercy on the part of the gods.

- Although the gods were occasionally good, merciful or just toward humans or toward one another, they were never consistently so.

- Humans were useful to the gods. They offered sacrifices to the gods and did nice things for them. The gods found men to be useful but expendable. They did not find men to be worthy objects of love, pity or mercy.

- In his role as god of justice, Zeus supervised justice in human actions toward other humans. He punished humans who broke their oaths or violated the guest-host relationship. This did not imply a just system between gods and humans or that gods treated humans fairly. It wasn't, and they often didn't.

- The anthropomorphic nature of the gods meant that they shared in humanity's less appealing emotions, as well as the more appealing ones. The gods could be cruel, spiteful and jealous. Frequently they were all of these.

- The gods knew a great deal, but they were not omniscient. They were very powerful, but they were not omnipotent. They were not outside or beyond the universe; they were part of the universe.

FROM SAVAGERY TO CIVILIZATION

This humankind creation myth, featuring Prometheus and Pandora, can be found in Hesiod's *Theogony* and his other book, *Works and Days* (both written at roughly the same time Homer wrote the *Iliad* and *Odyssey*).

MYTH OF THE FIVE RACES

A second creation myth, Myth of the Five Races, can also be found in Hesiod and is later repeated by Ovid. This second myth does not dovetail or agree with the Prometheus/Pandora version in any way. The two are completely different and in fact contradict one another. In this second account, Hesiod described five successive races of humans, starting with the Golden Race and ending with our own. The overall pattern of the five races is one of degeneration and increased hardship.

The first race, the *Golden Race*, was created by the immortals during the reign of Cronus, whom Zeus defeated in the war of the titans. This race had neither care nor troubles, and old age did not exist. They did not have to work for food. Since it was axiomatic that humans must die, the Golden Race eventually died out as well. They became benign spirits.

The *Silver Race,* also created by the gods, began a pattern of degeneration and was greatly inferior to the Golden Race. These humans lived as children, nourished by their mothers, for 100 years. Upon reaching adulthood, they lived a short while and were violent and irreverent. They refused to pay proper sacrifice to the gods. So Zeus destroyed the Silver Race.

Zeus created the *Bronze Race* from ash trees. They were a warlike and violent people. They used bronze for their weapons, homes and much else. They too died out, likely having killed each other off. Both the humans of this race and the handles of their spears were made from ash wood, which helps explain why they were so warlike.

The fourth race was the *Race of Heroes*. This race produced a higher-quality and more just human than those of the Bronze Race. They were heroes, created by Zeus. Hesiod called them demigods.

A hero or demigod had one parent, usually the father, who was a god. Heroes figured large in Greek myth, such as the tales surrounding the Trojan War and the questing hero myths about Heracles, Theseus and others. Being half human and thus mortal, the Race of Heroes died out; most descended into the underworld.

The fifth and worst race of humans — Hesiod's and, by implication, our own race — was the *Race of Iron*. Neither Hesiod nor Ovid mentioned a creator of this race (Prometheus played no role in this myth). The lot of the Iron Race was one of increasing hardship and toil. The only end in sight was that conditions that had been worsening would continue to worsen.

Human characteristics of the Iron Race include old age, disease and trouble. As the Iron Race continues to deteriorate, sons will not reverence their fathers, friends will not be trustworthy with one another, and brothers will fight brothers. Eventually shame and retribution will no longer effectively constrain human behavior. No controls on human activity will exist whatsoever.

Zeus will eventually destroy our race of mortals. When children are born already gray-haired — when the Iron Race knows nothing but old age — Zeus will destroy us all.

DEEP PESSIMISM ABOUT MAN'S DEVELOPMENT

These creation myths come from Hesiod, who wrote of the beginnings of the world. One feature is common to each legend – the idea of mankind's frailty in the face of near-certain destruction. Sometimes men brought calamity upon themselves by impiety or murderousness. At other times, events over which men had no control rained down destruction. Even in those times, Zeus could be a vindictive god. As we saw, he punished men not only for their misdeeds, but also for the deeds of Prometheus.

Prometheus, of course, was a heroic figure and a friend of mankind. He stubbornly rebelled against Zeus' terrible power. His personal sacrifice on behalf of humanity deserves our undying gratitude — for the fire that warms our hearths, but even more for the fire he shot through our imaginations. He taught us to imagine and create, to think strategically and to plan, and to use cunning and trickery to our advantage, especially when opposing powerful forces.

Although the story of Pandora seems to place women solely in a negative light, it actually reveals a dual attitude toward females. The good news is that women are irresistible. The bad news is that women cause all of men's woes. There you have it.

Such a story could only arise in a male-dominated culture. The traits stressed as inherent in women – treacherous hearts, lying tongues, withholders of sex – these traits are the natural weapons of a subjugated sex.

The myth of the five ages of man reveals a deep pessimism about man's development. While each generation of gods improved over the prior one, each new race of man deteriorated. The ancient Greeks, at least to Hesiod's thinking, had not yet come to believe that man is capable of evolving from savagery to civilization. And, truth be told, the jury may still be out.

HERACLES, PAN-HELLENIC GREEK HERO, captured Cerberus, a three-headed dog that guarded the entrance to Hades. Heracles was the triumphant human hero and, simultaneously, the human hero who suffered, died, and became a god.

CHAPTER IV
GREEK HEROES AND HEROIC QUESTS

THE GULF BETWEEN GODS WHO LIVE FOREVER AND HUMANS WHO MUST DIE WAS IMMENSE. The Greeks bridged that gap by creating and revering their heroes. They told and retold stories about them. They granted them immortality, singing songs of the honor and glory they had achieved.

Heroes were the result of couplings between the human and the divine. Zeus and other gods and goddesses frequently descended to Earth to have their way with beautiful human women and handsome men. Aphrodite, goddess of sexual passion, often urged them on.

The gods might take on a magical form. See the poem, "*Leda and the Swan*," by William Butler Yeats. In the poem, Zeus assumes the form of a wild swan and seduces Leda, a mortal woman. Their offspring is Helen, the most beautiful woman in the world.

Many of the offspring of these divine/human liaisons grew into the first heroes among humankind. With the aid of the gods, Greek heroes won many victories against vicious monsters and completed monumental tasks.

Many of these heroes founded family dynasties. Most notable were Theseus (hero of Athens), Heracles (all-purpose Pan-Hellenic hero), Perseus (legendary founder of Mycenae), Achilles (greatest warrior of the Trojan War), and Aeneas (founder of Roman civilization).

DEFINITION OF GREEK HERO

The English word hero descended directly from the Greek word hero and had three basic meanings in ancient Greek.

- A hero, or demigod, could refer to someone who lived in the past, particularly up to the time of the Trojan War.

- A hero could refer to a dead person who was revered and to whom sacrifices were offered. He was likely the protector of a particular site or city (often because he had founded it). He need not have been a good man, simply an extraordinary one.

- Or a hero could refer to a human who had one divine parent. Achilles, Heracles, and Theseus were all heroes in this sense. Odysseus, Agamemnon, and Oedipus were not.

The stories of heroes involve the notion, often found in myth, that things were different in the remote past. Their myths imply that, at one time, humans had greater powers than today that since have been lost.

CHARACTERISTICS OF A GREEK HERO

First, a Greek hero had an *unusual conception or birth*. Most famous heroes were the offspring of Zeus or Poseidon. Sometimes the parent was a goddess such as Aphrodite, mother of Aeneas, or Thetis, mother of Achilles. The actual births of heroes often involved strange complications.

Heroes were *born into royalty*. Heroes were almost always the offspring of a princess or queen. Typically, the god responsible for the hero either disguised himself as the husband of the queen, or the princess slept with a god and a mortal on the same night. Both the earthly and divine father invariably claimed him.

A prophecy would result in the hero being *abandoned at birth*. Upon the birth of a hero, the fates or the oracle often issued a prophecy. The prediction frightened the parents so badly that they abandoned the child in the wilderness. But since the heroic child was favored by the gods, someone other than his parents saved and raised him. Sometimes, through no fault of the parents, the child needed to be raised away from home.

Heroes performed *amazing feats at a young age*. Young heroes invariably demonstrated their abilities when very young. Heracles, for example, killed two giant snakes as a youngster. Theseus moved a huge rock and fought what he thought was a lion. Such events were harbingers of great things to come for the young heroes.

For obvious reasons, heroes were *favored by the gods*. A young hero, child of Zeus, would get help on a quest from his divine father or another Olympian. The gods would lend to the heroes special items such as helmets, winged sandals, and golden bridles.

Heroes would *embark upon heroic quests*. Heroes made the world a safer place. They defeated monsters, killed evil kings, or righted egregious wrongs. Heroes knew that they must die, so bards must sing songs that would perpetuate the stories of their great deeds.

The hero also *traveled to the underworld*. The hero had to confront death and return stronger and rejuvenated. Since heroes were mortal, confronting death allowed them to face their own mortality. The hero invariably *married a princess*, but rather than marital bliss, turmoil and unhappiness frequently ensued. And finally, the hero had *larger-than-life attributes*, but he also had larger-than-life flaws.

THESEUS, PROTECTOR OF ATHENS

Let's examine one myth in which many of these characteristics play a role – the myth of Theseus, protector of Athens.

During birth, childhood, and young adulthood, Theseus demonstrated typical heroic elements, some almost reminiscent of folktale. Oddities and ambiguities surrounded his conception. One was an apparent double-fatherhood. His human father was Aegeus, king of Athens. His mother, Aithra, was raped by Poseidon on the same night that she slept with Aegeus. Thus, the parentage of Theseus was uncertain.

The Greeks created a myth with a double fatherhood issue for one very good reason. Theseus was the great hero of Athens. As such, Athenian myth required him to be a top-notch hero. The father of a top-notch hero must be a god. So Theseus had to have a god as a father.

Theseus was also the most important legendary king of Athens. A Greek became king by inheriting the kingship from his father. So, Theseus had to have a father who was the king of Athens. Theseus had to fill both roles – a really top-notch hero with a god for a father, and a legitimate king of Athens with a king of Athens as a father. Thus Theseus was given two fathers.

FROM SAVAGERY TO CIVILIZATION

Before Theseus was born, Aegeus showed Aethra, Theseus' mother, a large rock under which he left his sandals and sword. He told her that if she gave birth to a boy, and if the boy grew strong enough to lift the rock, and if he recovered his father's sword and sandals from under the rock, then he should travel to Athens to claim his patrimony.

THESEUS, ATHENIAN HERO

Theseus grew up to be strong, athletic, courageous, and intelligent. Upon reaching manhood, he lifted the rock that his mother pointed out and reclaimed the sword and sandals. He set out for Athens to claim his patrimony.

Theseus purposefully traveled to Athens by the dangerous overland route, which was beset with monsters and robbers. He sought out all the challenges the local monsters might confront him with. For every offense done him, Theseus would mete out punishment exactly befitting that offense.

The bandits in the area tortured and murdered travelers in inventive ways. One clubbed his victims to death with an iron cudgel. Another made unlucky travelers wash his feet. He then kicked them off a cliff into the sea, where a man-eating turtle devoured them. And one bent two pine trees to the ground, tied his victims to the tree tops, and then released the trees.

The most famous bandit, Procrustes, was a rogue smith as well as a bandit. He tied his victims to an iron bed. If his victims were too long for the bed, he cut off their limbs to fit. If they were too short, he stretched them out.

Theseus destroyed each of these killers, using their own methods against them.

The purpose of Theseus' deeds of valor was to save Attica, the peninsula on which Athens is located. He cleared it of danger and made Attica safe for people to travel from one town to another. The mythic monsters and outlaws he overcame represented lawlessness, lack of political unity, and lack of safety on the roads. By wiping out the monsters, Theseus took the first big step to eventually unifying all of Attica under Athenian control.

GREEK HEROES AND HEROIC QUESTS

With tales of his exploits having preceded him, Theseus arrived in Athens and was proclaimed a hero. His father, King Aegeus, recognized as his own the sword that Theseus carried. He rejoiced to find he had such a distinguished son.

THESEUS AND THE MINOTAUR

Athens had a political problem at the time. To punish Athens for an ancient crime against Crete, King Minos of Crete had long demanded an annual tribute of seven maidens and seven youths. These were to be fed to the Minotaur, a human-eating monster with the head of a bull and the body of a man. The Minotaur lived in a labyrinth, an incredibly complex maze from which it was almost impossible to escape.

The time had come to pay the tribute of youths and maidens. Theseus joined the party of doomed young people. He planned to free Athens from the dreadful annual tribute to the Minotaur. Aegeus gave his son a black sail to be hoisted in case of disaster and a white one to use in case of victory. Theseus set sail for the island of Crete. The encounter of Theseus with the Minotaur and the help he received from the Cretan princess Ariadne, daughter of Minos, are the most famous elements of the myth about Theseus.

Upon Theseus' arrival in Crete, Ariadne fell in love with him and determined to help him. She obtained a ball of thread with which Theseus could find his way out of the maze once he had entered.

Armed with nothing but the thread, Theseus penetrated the labyrinth with his fellow victims. At length he came upon the Minotaur asleep, and vanquished him. By means of the thread, he led his companions to freedom.

The thread is often called the *clue of Ariadne*, and *clue* in English originally meant simply a *ball of yarn*. In modern usage, the word clue means the one element that leads you out of your perplexity to an understanding. This comes from the story of the clue of Ariadne.

Theseus promised to marry Ariadne. He took her with him as far as the island of Naxos. There, he either abandoned or simply forgot her. He then sailed for Athens, but forgot to take down the black sail and hoist the white one. His father Aegeus, who watched for the ship from a cliff, saw the black sail of defeat. He hurled himself into the sea in a fit of despair. And that's how the Aegean Sea got its name.

THESEUS, KING OF ATHENS

Theseus became king of Athens and took over the government. Under his wise supervision, a democracy was established. It included town council meetings and a popular vote. Theseus persuaded the small and independent towns of Attica to unify under one centralized control which was, of course, based in Athens. Theseus himself was commander in chief. He allowed the citizens to run things as they wished in the belief that political liberty made people more responsible and more prosperous.

Perhaps one reason Theseus set up a self-running form of government was that he found being a ruler to be oppressive. He preferred heroic and risky exploits. Over the ensuing years, Theseus had many more adventures. However, as he grew older, he found less and less pleasure in them. The Athenians became more and more quarrelsome. In the end he died a miserable death at the hands of his host, King Lycomedes, who pushed him from a cliff because of a territorial dispute. Eventually the Athenians erected a tomb for their hero.

THESEUS, FLAWED HERO

As a hero, Theseus enjoyed an outstanding beginning. His great exploits proved beneficial to others. In ridding the land route to Athens of robbers, he made the way safe for other travelers. In killing the Minotaur, he freed Athens of its obligatory human sacrifices. In giving Athens a democratic government, he made citizens out of subjects. He made a point of defending the weak.

Although Theseus was generous, brave, helpful, and intelligent, he had flaws that undermined his happiness. He suffered a tragic middle age, and his life was brought to a sad close.

How could that happen to a Greek hero after all the glorious achievements of his early years?

For one thing, his streak of rashness harmed him. His negligence in failing to hoist the white sail sent his father Aegeus hurtling from a cliff. That may have determined the manner of his own death, since he too died in such a fall. In abandoning, forgetting or neglecting Ariadne, he seemed to have laid a curse on his future marital attachments, which were unhappy affairs. And all of his adventuring seemed only to play out his own angry ignorance and overweening pride.

The Greeks understood human character. They grasped how a trait like ambition could turn from a virtue into a bane, and how a noble personality might have serious defects that lead to ruin. They regarded the exploits of Theseus as worthy of emulation. But they also knew that a price had to be paid for heroism, and they did not flinch at showing that price in their legends.

THESEUS, HERO OF ATHENS, SLAYS THE MINOTAUR, the human-eating monster with head of a bull and body of a man. Theseus escaped the labyrinthine home of the beast using the famous "clue of Ariadne."

FROM SAVAGERY TO CIVILIZATION

HERACLES, PAN-HELLENIC GREEK HERO

The greatest and most famous Greek hero of all was Heracles (Hercules to the Romans). He was the son of Zeus and the mortal woman Alcmene. Most Greek heroes were associated with only one city, but Heracles was a Pan-Hellenic hero, claimed by all of Greece. Heracles is mentioned in epic, tragedy, history, and most other genres of Greek and Roman literature.

Like those of many other heroes, Heracles' babyhood was unusual. Always-jealous Hera, Zeus' wife, hated the sons Zeus fathered with other women. She especially detested Heracles and sabotaged him from the day of his birth. But even as a baby, Heracles showed strength and courage. When Hera sent huge snakes to kill him in his cradle, the baby Heracles, instead of being frightened, strangled them.

When Heracles reached maturity, he manifested not only extreme strength and courage, but also other extreme characteristics. His bellowing rages made the earth tremble. His appetite for food and drink was insatiable. And his sexual appetite was inexplicably strong.

When Heracles was only 18 years old, he famously met the 50 daughters of Thespios. He slept with all 50 of them in the same night. (*We're also told that all 50 daughters became pregnant, and all 50 bore sons. When the 50 sons reached maturity, they formed the Worldwide Wrestling Federation.*)

Heracles' excessive rages sometimes boiled over into madness. In one especially notorious episode, perhaps caused by Hera, Heracles killed his own children by his first wife, and perhaps killed her as well.

TWELVE LABORS OF HERACLES

These murders by Heracles led directly to his famous 12 labors. On the advice of the oracle at Delphi, Heracles atoned for his crimes by performing all the labors his cousin Eurystheus ordered over 12 years. The Delphic priestess promised that if Heracles successfully accomplished the labors, he would atone for his crimes and be rewarded with immortality.

Heracles' 12 labors became increasingly difficult, and he had to travel increasingly greater distances to perform them. Every one of the

GREEK HEROES AND HEROIC QUESTS

labors would have been impossible, even fatal, for lesser men. Heracles accomplished them all. These were the 12 labors:

1. Kill the Nemean Lion, which was invulnerable to piercing wounds by arrow, spear, sword, or other sharp object. Heracles clubbed it to death, skinned it, and took the lion's skin as his cloak.

2. Kill the Lernaean Hydra – a snake with nine heads, one of which was immortal. When one head was cut off, two grew in its place. Heracles sought help from his nephew Iolaus. When Heracles cut off one of the hydra's heads, his nephew cauterized the neck to keep the head from growing back. When Heracles cut off the immortal head, he buried it under a boulder. Thus Heracles vanquished the hydra.

3. Capture the Cerynian Hind or golden-horned deer. While not dangerous itself, the hind was sacred to Artemis. She would have been angry if Heracles had injured it. Instead, Heracles captured the deer and delivered it alive to Eurystheus.

4. Capture the Eramanthian Boar. Heracles' task was to bring this savage beast back alive to Eurystheus. Which he did.

5. Clean the Augean Stables. This labor was difficult but not dangerous. The stables had never been cleaned. In order to flush them out, Heracles diverted two rivers to flow through the stables and wash them out. (*For this feat, Heracles was the first to be called a Stable Genius.*)

6. Kill the Stymphalian Birds. These creatures lived in a swamp and could shoot their arrow-sharp feathers from their wings. Heracles killed them all, either by shooting them with his bow and arrow or by slingshot.

The next three labors took place outside of Greece. They required Heracles to travel farther away, and the labors became progressively stranger.

7. Catch the Cretan Bull. The Cretan Bull was perhaps the same bull that sired the Minotaur that Theseus killed. Heracles caught it and brought it home to Eurystheus.

8. Tame the Mares of Diomedes. Heracles tamed these man-eating mares and then allowed them to eat Diomedes, their murderous master.

9. Steal the Belt of Hippolyta. Hippolyta was an Amazon queen. Her belt was an ornate sash. Heracles had to fight her, overcome her, and forcibly wrest the belt from her. He delivered the belt to Eurystheus.

The final three labors carried Heracles to the very edge of the world, the Far West. There, Heracles was pitted against emblems of mortality and immortality. Traveling to the Far West in Greek mythology equaled approaching the land of the dead.

10. Steal the Cattle of Geryon. Geryon was a triple-bodied monster living in the Far West. Heracles fought him, defeated him, stole his cattle, and drove them back home to Eurystheus.

11. Steal the Apples of the Hesperides. These three goddesses, daughters of Night, lived on an island in the Far West. On their island a tree, guarded by a dragon, blossomed with golden apples. With the help of Atlas, the titan who forever holds the sky upon his shoulders, Heracles retrieved the apples.

12. Capture Cerberus. In the final labor, Heracles descended into Tartarus to fetch back Cerberus, the three-headed guard dog of the underworld. This was the clearest example of Heracles being pitted against the forces of death. Heracles stole the guard dog, and in an emblematic conquest of death, presented the dog to Eurystheus.

Thus, Heracles completed the 12 labors, atoned for his crimes, and became eligible for immortality.

GREEK HEROES AND HEROIC QUESTS

HERACLES' PATH TO IMMORTALITY

Heracles is one of very few humans in Greek mythology to successfully achieve immortality and become a god. His achievement did not come about because of his exceptional goodness. Rather, Heracles became immortal because of his exceptional wrongdoing and, even more importantly, because of his exceptional suffering.

Heracles' marriage to his second wife Deianira was beset with difficulties. When, years later, Heracles fell in love with another woman, Deianira gifted him a robe that had been dipped in the poison blood of a centaur Heracles had killed. The robe burned Heracles' flesh but did not kill him. In agony, he mounted a funeral pyre and burned himself to death.

However, only Heracles' body died. His soul became a god, and he took his place on Mount Olympus. This is the fullest statement we have of an idea commonly found in Greek myth – an individual's rite of passage. A mortal human being must pass from initiation through suffering and death in order to be redeemed and become immortal. Here, after committing major crimes and suffering through nearly impossible 12 labors, Heracles achieved immortality by burning his mortal body, intentionally.

HERACLES EMBRACED DUALITY

Several polar opposites seem to underlie Heracles' myth. Heracles was:

- Admirable and horrifying, powerful and powerless.

- Both the hero who overcame monsters and marked out the civilized world, and also the madman who killed his wife and children.

- Supremely ill-fated and supremely fortunate.

- An all-too-human hero who achieved immortality and became a god.

- The hero who both resisted death and intentionally embraced it.

- The hero who conquered death in a sense with his last three labors. Yet his own death arrived through voluntary self-cremation. And finally,

- Both a serious, even tragic figure, but also a comic figure of excess.

Finally, Heracles was a kind of ***everyman*** figure. He contained within himself all human attributes and their opposites. **He clearly embraced the Dionysian tragic worldview:** *"Everything always has its opposite within itself."* Heracles, the greatest Greek hero, encompassed the greatest duality. **He became the triumphant human hero and, simultaneously, the human hero who suffered, died, and became a god.**

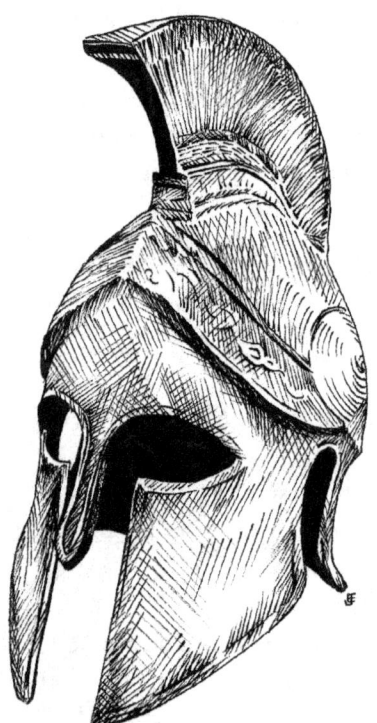

HELMET OF AN ANCIENT GREEK HERO.
Painful rites of initiation, suffering and death (or symbolic death), followed by atonement and resurrection to a higher plane – that was the tribal rite of passage required to immortalize a Greek hero.

CHAPTER V
BACKGROUND OF THE TROJAN WAR MYTH

THE TROJAN WAR WAS THE MOST FAMOUS EPISODE IN GREEK MYTHOLOGY, BUT WAS IT AN ACTUAL HISTORICAL EVENT? Debate has raged for centuries over that question. Did the city of Troy actually exist some 3000 years ago on the northwest corner of Anatolia (now Turkey)? Did the Trojans and Greeks fight a 10-year-long war there, from which the Greeks emerged victorious?

No hard evidence exists to support the notion of a real Trojan War as described by Homer. And yet over the years the veil of mystery surrounding Troy's real history has lifted a bit.

In 1868, archaeological excavations revealed that Troy – the city of myth and legend – did in fact exist. Further, a war most likely took place there at about the time of Homer's *Iliad*. What would have led to such a war?

Around the first millennium BC, Greece, supported by its peerless navy, was a military and economic powerhouse throughout the Mediterranean Sea region. The Greeks combined their commercial trade in gold and salt, among other trade goods, with their ongoing colonial expansion.

Also during that period, Troy had become an incredibly valuable piece of real estate. The Trojans controlled a vital choke point on the trading routes: the Hellespont (Dardanelles), which connect the Mediterranean to the Sea of Marmara and through it to the Black Sea. As a result, the Trojans held a monopoly on the Aegean Sea salt trade. For the Greeks, more than enough justification existed to warrant an invasion of Troy, and the Greeks probably did invade Troy more than once.

Of course, this is mostly conjecture. The true nature of Homer's Trojan War will probably never be known. It seems most likely that Homer melded together many threads of other tales and historical events to weave his epics.

FROM SAVAGERY TO CIVILIZATION

TROJAN WAR MYTH

Although the historical record is fuzzy, like looking through gauze, the mythic record reeks with the certainty of the faithful. The Greeks of the Classical Age, and later the Romans, firmly believed that the Trojan War was a real historical event. To them, it defined the end of the Heroic Age and the beginning of purely human history.

The Trojan War gazed Janus-like in two directions at once — backward to myth and the great Age of Heroes, but also forward into human society, since those heroes became the ancestors of their own great human families.

The entire story of the Trojan War was told in several ancient works of literature. The fullest descriptions are found, of course, in the *Iliad* and the *Odyssey*. They both deal with episodes that occurred either during or after the Trojan War.

The Roman epic, the *Aeneid* by Virgil, describes the sack of Troy at the war's end. The context and aftermath of the war were also crucially important subjects of the Greek tragedies that Aeschylus, Sophocles and Euripides wrote.

THE BASIC STORY

The basic story of the Trojan War – what happened, when, where and why – is simple. However, the many stories allied with it – the other myths that become connected to it – make it quite complex. Here's the basic story:

The Trojan prince Paris seduced and abducted the most beautiful woman in the world, Helen, daughter of Zeus and wife of Menelaus, king of Sparta. Paris ran away with Helen and took her back to Troy.

Under the command of Menelaus' elder brother, Agamemnon, the Greeks mustered an army to sail to Troy and fight for Helen's return. This war between the Greeks and Trojans lasted 10 years. The fighting was evenly balanced for most of those years. Each side had its foremost great warrior -- Achilles for the Greeks, Hector for the Trojans. Eventually, Achilles killed Hector.

Finally, the Greeks resorted to trickery to overcome the Trojans. Odysseus, the cleverest of the Greek heroes, famously invented the Trojan horse. Hiding their warriors in the belly of the horse, the Greeks gained access to the city. When night fell, they sacked Troy. The traditional date given for this event was 1184 BC.

JUDGMENT OF PARIS

The Trojan War myth attracted many related stories. One had to do with the birth of Achilles and its being, in effect, the first and foremost cause of the war. As the story goes, a prophecy about Achilles was given before he was even conceived.

Achilles' mother was Thetis, a sea-goddess or nymph. The prophecy said that she would bear a son who would be greater than his father. This meant that no god would risk mating with Thetis, no matter how desirable a woman she may have been. No god wanted a son who would overthrow him when the boy grew to maturity.

BRILLIANT ACHILLES, GREATEST GREEK WARRIOR. A fiercely uncompromising man of unbending principle, constant sorrow, and monstrous anger.

FROM SAVAGERY TO CIVILIZATION

To sidestep this problem, Zeus decided to marry Thetis off to a human being, Peleus. A human father would not be threatened by the idea that his son would be greater than himself.

However, Thetis was not happy with the idea of marrying a human. Goddesses viewed marriage to mortals, sexual relations with mortals, and bearing the children of mortals – all as degrading and disgusting.

WHO WAS THE FAIREST FEMALE?

In order to placate Thetis, Zeus hosted a magnificent wedding feast for her. He invited all the gods and goddesses to the wedding of Peleus and Thetis. Zeus didn't want any trouble, so he purposely did not invite Eris, the goddess who personifies strife and discord.

But his plan didn't work. Eris was offended at not being invited, and so she made trouble. She tossed a golden apple down on the banquet table, where all the goddesses and gods were seated. Inscribed on the apple were the words, *For the Fairest*. The goddesses Hera, Athena and Aphrodite all said, perhaps in unison, "*Ah, a gift for me. How nice.*" And each reached for the golden apple.

So, to whom was the golden apple finally awarded? One of those three goddesses had to be judged as the most beautiful. Rather than deciding himself, Zeus wisely delegated the job to a mortal. He tapped Paris, a Trojan prince and son of Priam, king of Troy, to judge among the three goddesses.

PARIS CHOSE BEST BRIBE

As it turned out, Paris didn't need to select the most beautiful goddess. Rather, he only had to accept the most appealing bribe.

- Hera, wife of Zeus, promised to make Paris lord of Europe and Asia; she offered political power.

- Athena, goddess of just war and wisdom, promised to make Paris the greatest warrior in the world. Through his prowess in battle, he would lead the Trojans to victory against the Greeks.

BACKGROUND OF THE TROJAN WAR MYTH

- Aphrodite, goddess of sexual passion, offered to make him an irresistible lover. She promised that the most beautiful woman in the world would be his.

So, to absolutely no one's surprise, Paris chose sexual pleasure over political power or power in battle. He awarded the golden apple to Aphrodite.

THOUSAND SHIPS LAUNCHED

As it happened, the most beautiful woman in the world was Helen, Menelaus' wife. Helen was the love/lust child of Zeus and the human woman Leda. (*Remember Yeats' poem "Leda and the Swan"? This is the same Leda.*)

So Paris traveled to Sparta and spent nine days as a guest under Menelaus' roof. During that time, Paris seduced and then kidnapped Helen and absconded with her to Troy.

Menelaus vowed to fight for his wife's return. Under the command of his older brother Agamemnon, the Greeks launched a thousand ships and sailed for Troy. (According to the *Iliad*, the actual number of ships was closer to 1200.)

This episode is known as the judgment of Paris, and according to the myth, it provided the immediate cause of the Trojan War. The entire episode occurred before the opening of the *Iliad*.

HOUSE OF ATREUS SEEKS REVENGE

The events leading up to the Trojan War were also closely connected in other ways with the brothers Agamemnon and Menelaus of the House of Atreus. Their story more or less developed along with the Trojan War story.

The most obvious connection was between the wives of the brothers: Helen, Menelaus' wife, and her half-sister Clytemnestra, Agamemnon's wife. The abduction of Helen, therefore, offended Menelaus as an individual and the entire Atreus family.

We cannot overstate how serious a crime Paris committed. It was a major offense against *xenia*, the Greek term for the *all-important guest-host relationship* in Greek culture. As a warmly welcomed guest in someone's home (as Paris was), one is absolutely prohibited from running off with the host's wife (which Paris did).

SACRIFICE OF IPHIGENIA

Agamemnon's fleet gathered at Aulis, a port on the east coast of Greece, before sailing for Troy. However, adverse winds detained them for an entire month. The fleet could not leave port. Agamemnon, as commander-in-chief, asked his seer, the prophet Calchas, to explain what was wrong.

Calchas told Agamemnon that Artemis, goddess of the hunt, was angry. (*Remember why? Because Agamemnon had killed her sacred deer and then boasted that he was a better hunter than the goddess.*) She demanded a sacrifice of Agamemnon's eldest daughter Iphigenia in order for the winds to blow favorably. Agamemnon obeyed. He sacrificed Iphigenia to placate the goddess. Then the winds did blow, and Agamemnon and his army sailed to Troy.

The Greek expedition to Troy thus began with a terrible act of impiety – the slaughter of a young girl by her father as though she were an animal. To the Greeks, human sacrifice was a dreadful act. Even though a goddess directly ordered the sacrifice of Iphigenia, a Greek human actually committed the crime. And a Greek human would pay dearly for it.

All of this occurred 10 years before the action of the *Iliad* began.

SACK OF TROY: SACRILEGES ABOUNDED

The Greeks began their expedition with a serious act of impiety – the sacrifice of Iphigenia. They also acted badly at the end of the war when they sacked Troy, which transpired after the action of the *Iliad* was over.

Among the outrages committed by the Greeks during the sack of Troy, some stand out:

- Priam, king of Troy, was an aged and venerable man and the father of Hector and Paris. Neoptolemos, the son of Achilles, slaughtered King Priam in front of his wife Hecuba while he grasped onto his household altar. According to the

Greeks' own cultural beliefs, Priam should have been safe from execution in that position.

- Priam's daughter, Cassandra, sought out a temple of Athena for refuge. Inside the temple, she embraced the statue of Athena. She should have been under Athena's care and protection. That cultural nicety, however, did not impede the Greek warrior, Ajax. He entered the temple, dragged Cassandra away from Athena's statue, and raped her in the temple. To the Greeks, this was about as horrible an outrage as one could imagine.

- Hector's baby son, Astyanax, was thrown from the city walls, as his mother Andromache watched.

- Finally, before the Greeks departed from the ashes of fallen Troy, they sacrificed Priam's young daughter, Polexena, to the ghost of Achilles. Thus the Greek expedition both began with the sacrifice of an innocent girl (Iphigenia) and ended with the sacrifice of an innocent girl (Polexena).

These many outrages angered the gods. They reacted by inflicting many hardships on the surviving Greeks as they suffered their way home. When Agamemnon arrived home, his wife Clytemnestra axed him to death. Ajax drowned at sea. Odysseus spent 10 years wandering – a total of 20 years away from his home on Ithaca. Menelaus and Helen were blown off course and landed in Egypt. They idled away seven years there before finally reaching Sparta.

From the Romans' perspective, the most important story about surviving Trojans was that of Aeneas, son of Aphrodite and Anchises, and also a cousin of Hector. According to the *Iliad*, Aeneas was destined to survive the Trojan War and found another city in the West. The Romans seized upon those lines in the *Iliad* and made them their own. Thereafter, Romans asserted that Aeneas made his way to Italy after the war and became the ancestor of Roman civilization.

GODS' COMMANDS VS INDIVIDUAL RESPONSIBILITY

In all of these connected stories, we see the complex interaction between the gods' commands and individual human responsibility. The individual is responsible for the actions he takes, whether a god has commanded them or not.

Although the war was caused by several individuals, especially Paris, all of the actions taken by those individuals were sanctioned by the gods. And so the individuals could rightfully claim that they had no choice. Paris abducted Helen because the goddess Aphrodite told him that Helen was his rightful wife.

However, the goddess' command did not absolve Paris of his guilt – guilt that accrued to him for severely violating the guest-host relationship, stealing his host's wife. Moreover, his society was not absolved of that guilt either. The entire Trojan society suffered terrible repercussions because of Paris' misdeed, despite the fact that Aphrodite told him to do it.

The case of Agamemnon's sacrifice of his daughter Iphigenia is similar. This was a terrible transgression — the worst thing a father could possibly do. But he could correctly claim that the goddess Artemis commanded him to do it. That was true but irrelevant. Agamemnon was not absolved of guilt. There would be hell to pay for this crime, as the plays of Aeschylus dramatize.

So, if the gods commanded a mortal to commit a transgression, or if he seriously violated man-made rules of proper behavior, he would be held to account by both men and the gods for his actions — not his intentions, excuses, or motivations, but his actions.

Now add to all of this the concept of fate — that individuals may have been fated to perform actions that were wrong (think Oedipus the King). The picture becomes even more complex. **For even those who were fated to commit transgressions were still held responsible for their actions. To the Greeks, individual motivations were of trivial importance; individual actions were everything.**

CHAPTER VI
THE ILIAD BY HOMER

Most of the Trojan War myth is not found in the Iliad. The back story of the House of Atreus is not. The judgment of Paris episode is not. The sacrifice of Agamemnon's daughter Iphigenia is not. The Trojan horse deception and the sack of Troy are not. All those stories are important elements of the Trojan War myth. None is found in the *Iliad*.

OPENING LINES; CRITICAL THEMES

In fact, the *Iliad* covers only a two-week period toward the end of the 10-year Trojan War. In the opening lines, Homer tells us what the *Iliad* is about:

> *Rage — Goddess, sing the rage of Peleus' son Achilles,*
> *murderous, doomed, that cost the Achaeans countless losses,*
> *hurling down to the House of Death so many sturdy souls,*
> *great fighters' souls, but made their bodies carrion,*
> *feasts for the dogs and birds,*
> *And the will of Zeus was moving toward its end.*
> *Begin, Muse, when the two first broke and clashed,*
> *Agamemnon lord of men and brilliant Achilles.*
> — Book I, Lines 1-8. Robert Fagles translation.

The *Iliad* is about the rage or wrath of Achilles – it's the very first word of the epic, and it's spoken twice in the first line – *menis* in Greek. Achilles is the son of Thetis, an immortal sea-goddess, and Peleus, a mortal man. Thetis made Achilles almost completely invulnerable at birth by dipping him in the River Styx. This rendered Achilles immortal everywhere except his heel, where Thetis held him. Thus the famous phrase to mean a point of weakness – an *Achilles' heel*. (This episode is not in the *Iliad* either.)

Achilles is without question the greatest warrior in the Greek expedition. He belongs to an aristocratic warrior society of Greek heroes, who are focused on battlefield achievement and its rewards.

These heroes – superior men descended from both gods and mortals – reign at the top of Greece's hierarchical social structure. The most prominent of these heroes is Achilles.

The word used for Achilles' wrath – *menis* – normally refers only to the gods. Homer applies *menis* to a man, as the very first word of the poem. It signifies the special difference Achilles represents among heroes. He becomes so outraged that he withdraws from the fighting and leaves his fellow Greeks to suffer great losses at the hands of the Trojans.

So, in the first few lines, Homer states, immediately and abruptly, the epic's critical themes – the wrath of Achilles; the suffering of his fellow Greeks; the will of Zeus (that the Greeks will win the war); and the quarrel between Agamemnon and Achilles.

This anger also becomes the narrative device by which Homer examines broader themes, such as mortality, the human condition, and how the warrior ethos affects what it means to be human.

AGAMEMNON AND ACHILLES QUARREL

The epic begins in the middle of things, *in media res* in Latin. Homer could assume that his audience knew the stories and the characters. The reader is carried to where the trouble originally arose, which is where the story of the *Iliad* actually begins: in the middle of war.

The action of the epic opens with a quarrel between Achilles and Agamemnon. The confrontation brings the reader immediately face-to-face with the Greek warrior ethos. Agamemnon, while king in his own land, was simply the leader, or commander-in-chief, of the expedition here.

During one of the Greek army's many raids of neighboring villages, the soldiers capture two beautiful enemy maidens, Chryseis and Briseis. The troops award these girls to Agamemnon and Achilles. Chryses, the father of Chryseis, pleads for her return, but Agamemnon denies the plea, in violation of accepted honorable behavior. Consequently, Chryses seeks recourse in a prayer to the god Apollo. Apollo punishes Agamemnon by inflicting a plague upon the Greek camp.

THE ILIAD BY HOMER

On the tenth day of the plague, Achilles calls an assembly of the army and asks the soothsayer, Calchas, to tell the cause of Apollo's anger. Calchas reveals that the plague exists because Agaememnon refuses to return Chryseis to her father. This infuriates Agamemnon. He has been publicly named as being responsible for the plague. He counters that if he is forced to surrender Chryseis, his rightful war prize, then he must be repaid with Achilles' war prize, Briseis.

ACHILLES' RAGE ERUPTS

Now it's Achilles' turn to be stunned and infuriated. In full view of all the soldiers, Agamemnon has demanded that Briseis be turned over to him. Keeping Briseis, according to Agamemnon, would render Achilles a public disgrace. Achilles refuses to accept this indignity. He announces that he will withdraw his troops from battle. He will not fight, and, furthermore, he and his men will return to their own country as soon as possible.

Achilles also prays to his mother, Thetis, to use her influence with Zeus. She asks Zeus to allow Trojan armies to start winning battles over the Greeks, at least for a time. Achilles hopes that Agamemnon will be disgraced if his army starts losing. He will be forced to repay the wrong he has done to Achilles, so that Achilles will reenter the war.

At the behest of Thetis, Zeus allows the Trojans to gain a temporary ascendancy in battle, until the Trojan forces reach the Greek ships at the sea's edge.

GODS INFLUENCE THE FATE OF HUMANS

For the first time in the epic, we get a glimpse of the relationship between gods and men. The gods take an active role in human affairs. Zeus metes out a kind of rough justice, one often much harsher than seems warranted.

The intervention of the gods in human affairs seems to imply that the gods can influence the fate of humans. The definition of fate is the allotted time of one's death. Can Zeus change one's ultimate fate or the timing of it? The answer is no. But he can certainly wreak havoc with the process of getting there.

For example, the gods know (although humans do not know) that Troy is fated to lose this war. Zeus cannot alter that ultimate fate. But events that occur before the final fall of Troy are subject to external influences. In this case, Zeus does change things. He allows Troy to win battles over the Greeks, for a while.

WHY GREEK HEROES WAGED WAR - TIMÊ AND KLEOS

But why does Achilles become so angry? Some have suggested that all that rage over a slave girl is the overreaction of an arrogant and spoiled brat.

Are you saying that the great warrior Achilles whines just because Agamemnon has taken away Briseis? Surely, slave girls galore bustle about Achilles' tent. Will he really abandon his fellow warriors and go home over this incident?

In short, does the taking of Achilles' war prize by Agamemnon really amount to a public disgrace? The answer is yes. In ancient Greek culture, this would have been a major humiliation. And so no, Achilles does not overreact.

To understand why Achilles' wrath is not an overreaction, we must understand the Homeric hero's motivations for fighting. Why does the Homeric warrior go to war in the first place? In this case, certainly, the Greek warrior fights to help regain Helen for Menelaus, but more important individual reasons exist for a Homeric hero to wage war.

Generally, the Homeric warrior goes into battle for two reasons. The first is to achieve *timê*, often translated as *gaining honor*. *Timê*, (pronounced teé-may), at its essence is tangible, physical expressions of honor in the form of booty, gifts, and slaves, especially slave girls.

Homeric warriors also fight to achieve *kleos*, or *everlasting, imperishable glory or fame*. In its most basic sense, *kleos* means *what other people speak aloud about you*, especially after you're dead. *Kleos* is the only immortality available to the Homeric warrior. Although the gods live forever, humans die. And so, in a preliterate society, achieving *kleos* is of existential importance. Every major warrior strives to achieve it. Yet, paradoxically, in order for the Homeric warrior to achieve *kleos*, someone always must die – either the warrior himself or his enemy. Throughout the epic, we are confronted with the paradoxical nature of *kleos* – immortal fame gained only through acts of death.

Furthermore, *timê* and *kleos* are closely related. The *kleos* one enjoys depends on the *timê* offered by one's peers. Homeric heroes fight to achieve both *timê* and *kleos*.

And that's why the withdrawal of Achilles from battle is such a devastating decision – for the prospects of the Greek army certainly, but also for Achilles himself. Without exploits, Achilles cannot achieve *timê* or *kleos*. Therefore, he has no identity. He can only sit in his shelter singing about fame and glory, but not achieving them. He can no longer be considered the best of the Greeks.

Achilles' withdrawal from battle results in his *timê* and by extension his *kleos* both being severely diminished. Honor accruing to Achilles and his ability to keep his reputation alive after his death significantly suffer. Achilles has suffered a grave dishonor, and now his entire worth as a human being has been called into question.

THE TROJAN PERSPECTIVE

In the Trojans, the Greek army finds a worthy opponent.

The Trojans are not portrayed as villains in the *Iliad*. Rather, for them, the war is a terrible tragedy, and one they never sought. The Trojans certainly fight for *timê* and *kleos*, as almost all Homeric warriors do. More importantly, though, they battle for their lives and their country's survival. We know from the first lines of the epic that the Trojans are fated to lose this war, but the Trojans don't know that. They fight to prevent defeat.

PARIS AND HELEN: TRUE LOVE

But let's remind ourselves: What is the specific *casus belli* (Latin for cause of war) that drives the Trojans to take up arms? They war on behalf of, and to defend, the adulterous affair between Paris and Helen.

We already observed Paris in action during the famed judgment of Paris that occurred outside the pages of the *Iliad*. Paris is a lover not a fighter — a behavioral strain he maintains in the *Iliad*.

Paris is unskilled and cowardly. Early in the epic, Hector arranges a duel to be fought between Paris, Helen's abductor, and Menelaus, Helen's husband. Hector seeks to end the war by forcing the primary opponents to face each other.

In this confrontation, Paris does not shine. He first runs away from the fight. Then, when Paris returns, Menelaus trounces him. Fortunately for Paris, Aphrodite spirits him away to the arms of Helen, before Menelaus can kill him.

Paris' brother Hector scolds and belittles him (hence our word *hector*), after he runs away from the duel. It could have ended the war. Paris admits that he does poorly in face-to-face combat. He does not live or fight by the Homeric code of honor shared by other heroes. Rather, Paris prefers shooting the bow and arrow – from a very long distance away. From beginning to end, by Greek standards, Paris is not much of a man. No hero, he.

What about Helen? Like Paris, Helen is a motivating force behind the war. When she ran off with Paris, leaving her husband behind, she acted like a god – forever unaccountable and indifferent. The possibility of consequences did not occur to her, just as it never occurs to the gods. Helen never considered that war would come to Troy because of her and Paris' actions, and that death in that war would be on both their hands.

But now, nearly 10 years later, as the *Iliad* opens, Helen has become more aware of the misery she has caused. She now understands that she's not a god and therefore unaccountable for her actions. Rather, she is a human being and must take responsibility. Gods don't do that; only humans do that.

So Helen accepts responsibility. She balks when, in Book III, the goddess Aphrodite urges her to go to bed with Paris one more time. In that scene, for perhaps the first time, Helen separates herself from divine indifference. She becomes human and feels the sorrow no human can escape. Helen's sorrow helps explain her bitter mocking words to Paris, after he loses the duel with Menelaus:

> *So, home from the wars!*
> *Oh would to God you'd died there, brought down*
> *By that great soldier, my husband long ago.*
>   — Book III, Lines 499-501. Robert Fagles translation.

Helen now despises Paris as much as everyone else does. The entire war now appears even more futile and senseless. Everyone recognizes the chasm of difference between what the Trojans risk (the total destruction of their culture), and what they risk it for (Paris and Helen's adulterous affair).

HECTOR, BREAKER OF HORSES

Now, after years of fierce fighting by both armies, Troy finds itself in dire straits. It will survive this war only through the devotion, courage and leadership of one man, Hector, son of King Priam. His epithet is *breaker of horses*. He is a formidable warrior – indeed the most formidable Greek or Trojan on the battlefield, except for Achilles.

But war is not Hector's native element. Unlike Achilles, he is a man made for peace. He fosters human relationships with sympathy, persuasion or kindness. And when firmness is necessary, he expresses firmness in forms of law that rest on granted authority.

Hector appears most himself in his relationships with others. Significantly, our first view of him in action is not in combat, but in an attempt to stop combat – when he arranges the duel between Paris and Menelaus.

HECTOR WITH WIFE AND SON

But Hector's relationships with his fellow countrymen and his family demonstrate his true quality. He visits his wife and son before returning to fight. He finds Andromache on the city walls, with their child Astyanax.

Andromache weeps and begs Hector to be careful, as wives have begged their husbands throughout history. She pleads with him to stop fighting hand-to-hand at the front line. Rather, he should command his troops from the safety of the walls.

But Hector can't do it. He is the Trojans' leader. He must fight in the front ranks. Here is Hector's sad reply:

All this weighs on my mind too, dear woman.
But I would die of shame to face the men of Troy
And the Trojan women trailing their long robes
If I would shrink from battle now, a coward.

— Book VI, Lines 522-25. Robert Fagles translation.

Hector's meeting with Andromache and Astyanax, wife and child, brings home the human cost of war. Being human, Hector does not know the future, or how the war will end. But he senses the worst in his gut. He will be killed by Achilles, Astyanax will be thrown from the walls of Troy, and Andromache will be led away into slavery.

ACHILLES' RAGE INTENSIFIES

The war of late has been going badly for the Greeks, as Zeus had promised. The Greeks sadly and the Trojans happily feel the impact of Achilles' absence from the battlefield.

Finally, in order to persuade Achilles to return to battle, Agamemnon sends emissaries to plead with him. They will tell Achilles of Agamemnon's admission of guilt in the affair of the slave girl Briseis. On Agamemnon's behalf, they will offer Achilles a magnificent recompense. The three emissaries, led by Odysseus, will attempt to persuade Achilles to accept Agamemnon's admission of guilt and his gifts, and return to battle.

All to no avail. Achilles rejects their offers in a long, passionate outburst. He pours out all the resentment stored up so long in his heart. He says he will hear no more speeches. Neither for Agamemnon nor for the Greeks will Achilles fight again.

In response to the embassy's pleading, Achilles says, "*I loathe his gifts.*" Nothing will change Achilles' mind, he says, "*Until he pays me back, pays full measure for all his heartbreaking outrage!*"
— Book IX, Lines 472-473. Robert Fagles translation.

However, most importantly, Achilles shocks his listeners to their core when he says this:

> *... What lasting thanks in the long run*
> *For warring with our enemies, on and on, no end?*
> *One and the same lot for the man who hangs back*
> *And the man who battles hard. The same honor waits*
> *For the coward and the brave. They both go down to Death.*
> *The fighter who shirks, the one who works to exhaustion.*
> *And what's laid up for me, what pittance? Nothing —*
> *And after suffering hardships, year in, year out,*
> *Staking my life on the mortal risks of war.*
> — Book IX, Lines 383-391. Robert Fagles translation.

Do not doubt it. Achilles' speech is almost unimaginably shocking. This is a change of seismic proportions – an abrupt about-face from thousands of years of Greek honor code behavior. Achilles' speech undercuts the entire basis of his society and the warrior culture. In effect, he says that *timé* (battle honor) and *kleos* (imperishable glory) are no longer important to him. He doesn't care about them any longer. Achilles rejects the Greek hero's warrior ethos.

ACHILLES' REJECTS TIMÊ AND KLEOS

Achilles' snub of Agamemnon's offer is a major turning point in the epic. Until now, one could sympathize with Achilles, because Agamemnon was clearly in the wrong. But Agamemnon has now offered honorable terms, and Achilles has rejected them. Achilles has put his injured pride above all other considerations. The moral balance begins to fall against him.

Nothing will satisfy Achilles now except Agamemnon's complete humbling – an unreasonable and unwarranted demand. Achilles' desire for revenge against Agamemnon overwhelms his better judgment and his loyalty to his friends.

More importantly and critical to the outcome of the epic, Achilles rejects *timê* and *kleos*. These are bedrock concepts of the heroic code of honor that the Greeks hold so dear. In a supreme expression of his own individuality, Achilles refuses to conform his behavior to the centuries-old tenets of the code of honor.

Achilles' rejection of the mores of his society exposes far-reaching implications. In effect, Achilles questions his world's entire paradigm of what it means to be human. Suddenly, in stark relief, there arises one of the central themes of the *Iliad* – the human condition. If it doesn't matter whether one achieves imperishable glory by dying or killing the enemy in battle, then what does mortality mean? Shall we prepare for certain death, simply accept it, or what? How do we come to terms with death?

These challenges lie at the heart of what it means to be human. Indeed, the resolution of the entire epic turns on whether or not Achilles can finally understand what it means to be human, whether he can accept that he is human, and whether he accepts that he will die.

Nevertheless, Achilles' rejection is reported back to Agamenon.

The embassy was a failure. As Book IX closes, the situation of the Greeks remains desperate.

THE DEATH OF PATROCLUS

The war resumes. One very long day is described in Books XI through XVIII – roughly a third of the entire poem. The action follows the standard give-and-take of battle, with courage and desperate fighting on both sides.

Zeus fulfills his promise to Thetis. The day belongs to Hector and the Trojans. They drive the Greeks back onto their ships. Throughout this long day, Achilles refuses to fight.

But Patroclus, Achilles' close friend and companion, tries to persuade Achilles to enter the battle. Failing that, Patroclus receives permission to enter the battle himself. He wants to fight, and he asks to wear Achilles' armor.

Achilles lends his armor and chariot to Patroclus, but warns him to drive the Trojans back from the Greek camp and no more. He should not push all the way to the walls of Troy. Achilles prays to Zeus to let Patroclus fight gloriously and return safely. Homer comments, *"The father granted him one prayer, but denied the other."*

Patroclus kills many Trojans but ignores Achilles' advice. He rushes to the wall of Troy and tries to climb it. Finally, Hector slays Patroclus. He strips Achilles' armor from the body of Patroclus and puts it on himself. All too soon Achilles hears the news from the battlefield. Patroclus is dead. The armies are fighting over his corpse.

The death of Patroclus is another critical turning point in the *Iliad*. It changes everything, again. The focus of the epic's narrative changes. Overwhelmed as he is by grief, Achilles himself changes. Most importantly, the object of Achilles' wrath changes — from Agamemnon to Hector.

Achilles is given his final chance to decide his own fate, for Thetis tells him he will die if he avenges Patroclus. Despite this knowledge, Achilles chooses revenge. Patroclus was his closest friend, a lesser reflection of his own glory. He realizes that Patroclus' death is his fault. He is angry with himself as well as with the Trojans. He will punish the Trojans. He will vent his all-consuming rage against Hector. Perhaps then he can assuage his own sense of guilt and grief.

THE ILIAD BY HOMER

ACHILLES AND HECTOR: POLAR OPPOSITES

Achilles makes peace with Agamemnon and returns to battle. His mother tells him that he is fated to die shortly after Hector dies. Achilles accepts his fate.

The next morning, the two champions come face-to-face at last. The contrast between them cannot be more striking. In many ways, Achilles and Hector are polar opposites. This will be a clash between two diametrically opposed world views.

Hector represents hearth, home, and city-state. He defends the principles of individual self-control and a constructive, positive way of life. Hector is a fully realized human being, connected with his family and his community.

Achilles, by contrast, personifies primitive brutality, anti-social destructiveness, and undisciplined instinct. Achilles is inhumanly isolated, cut off from family, friends, and community.

The two heroes are opposites in their knowledge of the future and in their attitude toward death. Hector is humanly fallible and can't even know his fate. He often misunderstands, disregards, or overlooks prophecies. Throughout the *Iliad*, he merely hopes, against growing evidence to the contrary, that one day he and his family will get out of this war alive.

On the other hand, Achilles' special knowledge of his two possible fates marks him out as different from most humans. After Patroclus' death, he knowingly chooses death for himself.

HECTOR DIES; ACHILLES DEFILES

The two also have opposite motivations for entering battle. Hector prefers not to battle at all. But he will fight to defend his city and people and for honor. Thus, Hector subordinates his individual desires for the good of his society.

Achilles at first refuses to fight because of the personal injury done him by Agamemnon. When he does enter the fray, he is driven only by revenge – to avenge the death of Patroclus. He no longer fights for heroic honor. Achilles overvalues the importance of one individual.

Hector's humanity and Achilles' inhumanity are highlighted in Book XXII. When the fight begins, Hector considers retreating. He is terrified. He flees from Achilles. He feels like he's in a nightmare. Achilles is described as looking like the *lord of battles*.

When Hector stops running, he proposes to Achilles that each one promise to return the other's body to his people. Achilles refuses. After Hector is wounded, he begs Achilles not to defile his body. Achilles' response is brutal. He even threatens cannibalism.

And so Hector dies. Achilles exults over his fallen enemy. His words make clear that he fought for himself alone. This is the satisfaction of a personal hatred. He is still cut off from humanity, a prisoner of his own self-esteem.

Achilles has traveled a bleak road: from understandable anger at the hands of Agamemnon; to rejection of the Homeric code of honor; to excessive rage over the death of Patroclus; to now uncontrollable and all-consuming rage in his treatment of the body of Hector. He defiles Hector's body, dragging it behind his chariot back and forth before the walls of Troy. King Priam and Hecuba, Hector's father and mother, stare in horror from the walls. His wife Andromache faints at the sight.

Achilles holds a magnificent funeral for Patroclus. On each of the nine days after the funeral, Achilles in his chariot circles Patroclus' funeral pyre, dragging Hector's body behind.

Finally, Zeus and the other gods determine that Hector's body must be returned to his family for a suitable burial. This will be done.

PRIAM AND ACHILLES WEEP TOGETHER

That night, escorted by the messenger god Hermes, King Priam, Hector's father, enters the Greek camp, unseen. He seeks out Achilles. He appeals to him as a suppliant, kneeling and clasping Achilles' knees. Priam offers Achilles a rich ransom for the return of Hector's body. He reminds Achilles of the feelings that he, Achilles, had for his own dead father, Peleus.

He kisses Achilles' hands. Priam's plea ends with these tragic and famous lines:

THE ILIAD BY HOMER

> *"I have endured what no one on earth has ever done before —*
> *I put to my lips the hands of the man who killed my son."*
> — Book XXIV, Lines 590-91. Robert Fagles translation.

Achilles reacts with wonder, compassion, and grief to these memories of home and parents that Priam's supplication has re-awakened. He begins to break out at last from his prison of self-absorbed, godlike passion. He accepts Priam's offer of ransom for Hector's body.

The two enemies weep together, Priam for Hector and Achilles for Patroclus, as well as for his father Peleus. Achilles comforts Priam by referring to the mixed good and evil that Zeus bestows on all humans, and telling him that he too must bear adversity.

KING PRIAM BEGGED ACHILLES FOR
THE BODY OF HIS SON HECTOR.
Achilles had killed Hector and defiled his body. The two men – warrior and suppliant king — wept together. Why did Achilles weep?

Achilles assumes the role of the old king's protector. He has dinner prepared and provides Priam with a bed for the night. He even oversees the preparations of Hector's body. He grants the Trojans an 11-day truce – sufficient time to conduct Hector's funeral rites.

Until the moment Priam pleaded with Achilles to release his son's body, Achilles had undergone no real change of heart during his years as a Greek warrior. He learned no moral lesson from his experiences. His meeting with Priam, however, marks a crucial moment in Achilles' moral development.

In their conversation, Achilles reveals the full depth of his affection for Patroclus. He also demonstrates his ability to understand another man's sorrow. He begins to see himself as another man might see him. The more humane and nobler side of his character begins to gain influence.

By relenting and restoring Hector's body to Priam, Achilles obeys the will of the gods and experiences a moral rehabilitation. He is changed and chastened. In some mysterious way, seeing his enemy's grief moves Achilles to recognize that he too must accept his own humanity.

THE ILIAD'S CLOSING EPISODE

In the *Iliad's* closing episode, the wrath of Achilles is finally assuaged. Hector is about to be buried. Achilles himself is about to die. The great antagonists of the epic have laid down their arms forever. The dramatic story of the wrath of Achilles and its effects has at long last been resolved.

It's important to note that the poet does not conclude his poem with a major historical event, such as the death of Achilles or the fall of Troy. Rather, he closes with the beginning of Achilles' rehabilitation and a simple act of kindness.

The epic began with a wrong deed committed by Agamemnon toward a suppliant father (Chryses). The epic concludes with a right deed done by Achilles toward another suppliant father (Priam). Achilles' kindness toward Priam sweeps away the remnants of his warrior's wrath and brings the work full circle.

Both the opening and closing episodes of the *Iliad* draw the reader's attention away from the state of play in the ongoing Trojan War. That's because the *Iliad* is not at its essence a war story. From beginning to end, the war situation essentially does not change. Rather, the opening and closing episodes focus on the tragic course of Achilles' rage to his final recognition of human values. That's the epic's central theme, worked out against a background of relentless violence and death.

The *Iliad* remains a terrifying poem. Achilles, just before his death, is redeemed as a human being after a career of violence and death. Perhaps Achilles' redemption offers some consolation and a few drops of dramatic satisfaction.

But then recall the tragic death of Hector, a fully realized human being and exemplar of human values his entire life. For the loss of Hector, there is neither consolation nor dramatic satisfaction.

Instead, we are left with a sense of waste. The scale continually descends toward loss. The *Iliad* remains not only the greatest epic poem in literature, but also the most tragic.

And it is fitting that the last line of the epic refers to the *burial* of a fully realized human being:

"*And so the Trojans buried Hector, breaker of horses.*"
— Book XXIV, Line 944. Robert Fagles translation.

ODYSSEUS gazed longingly across the sea toward his island home of Ithaca. The goddess CALYPSO had detained him for seven years. She wanted him to stay with her and become immortal. He insisted on living the life of a mortal.

CHAPTER VII
THE ODYSSEY BY HOMER

WHEN HOMER WROTE THE ODYSSEY, HE COULD ASSUME THAT HIS AUDIENCE WAS COMPLETELY FAMILIAR WITH THE ILIAD, as well as the closely related events that occurred before and after the Trojan War.

The word *nostos* is Greek for *homecoming* or *return*, and the source of our word *nostalgia*. Epic can be divided into *kleos* epic and *nostos* epic, or war epic and peace epic. *Nostos* is a major theme of the *Odyssey*, just as *kleos* is a major theme of the *Iliad*. *Kleos* is still very important in the *Odyssey*, but successfully achieving kleos no longer depends on death in battle. A hero can achieve kleos in peacetime and still remain alive.

Like the *Iliad*, the *Odyssey* begins in the middle of things. Also like the *Iliad*, Homer announces the subject of his companion epic in the opening lines:

> *Sing to me of the man, Muse, the man of twists and turns*
> *driven time and again off course, once he had plundered*
> *the hallowed heights of Troy.*
> *Many cities of men he saw and learned their minds,*
> *many pains he suffered, heartsick on the open sea,*
> *fighting to save his life and bring his comrades home.*
> *But he could not save them from disaster, hard as he strove —*
> *the recklessness of their own ways destroyed them all,*
> *the blind fools, they devoured the cattle of the Sun*
> *and the Sungod blotted out the day of their return.*
> *Launch out on his story, Muse, daughter of Zeus,*
> *start from where you will – sing for our time too.*
> — Book I, Lines 1-12. Robert Fagles translation.

The *Odyssey* begins 10 years after the end of the Trojan War. In the opening lines, Homer sketches out Odysseus' history and places him on Calypso's island.

He identifies Odysseus (Ulysses to the Romans) in the very first line by the epithet *polutropos*, here translated as *man of many turns*.

FROM SAVAGERY TO CIVILIZATION

No single English word corresponds precisely to *polutropos*, but it connotes a man who is wily, clever, resourceful, devious, sly, and perhaps all of these together. *Polutropos* as a descriptor connects us with the type of epic hero Odysseus is. It evokes the story of a man who's been blown about upon the sea and faced trials of every sort.

Just as the first word of the *Iliad* is wrath, indicating the warfare subject matter of the entire poem, so too, the first word of the Odyssey is *andra*, Greek for *man*. *Andra* is the subject matter of the *Odyssey*: one man, his adventures, and his struggles to get home. After briefly summarizing Odysseus' adventures after the fall of Troy, the poet suddenly leaves him and takes a side journey to Ithaca, Odysseus' home island. Odysseus does not actually appear in the *Odyssey* until Book V.

The first four books, called the *Telemacheia*, are mostly about Odysseus' son, Telemachus, and events at home on Ithaca. Spending these early pages on Ithaca provides a full sense of how badly Odysseus is needed at home, having been gone 20 years. His absence has caused great problems for his family. By his failure to return, both his wife Penelope and son Telemachus are left in limbo. Their proper courses of action are unclear.

Penelope does not know whether she's a wife or a widow. Thus she has two conflicting duties. If she is a wife, she must be loyal to her absent husband, continue to manage their household affairs, and not remarry. However, unmarried women have no place in Greek culture. So, if she is a widow, she must remarry.

Telemachus is about 21 years old. He doesn't know whether he should guard the kingdom on behalf of his father, or, since he is just coming of age, assert his own right to be king of Ithaca. And what should he do about the suitors who loll about the palace, waiting and hoping to marry Penelope?

SUITORS SPREAD SOCIAL DISARRAY

The suitors of Penelope are the focal point of all this disarray on Ithaca and in Odysseus' home. As suitors, they destroy Odysseus' household and threaten his marriage. Implicit in their persistence is the idea that whoever marries Penelope will become ruler of

Ithaca. Thus, they also threaten the rights of Telemachus to inherit the throne. The suitors' wanton disregard of the sacred guest-host relationship is evidence of the disordered state of the island.

Homer opens the *Odyssey* at the precise moment when the situation on Ithaca has become most dire. Telemachus is near the age to claim his right to be king. He should assert himself as master of his household. Penelope has used a trick to fend off the more than 100 suitors (actually 108) who have invaded the royal palace for three years.

Claiming it as part of her filial duty, by day she weaves a shroud for the eventual funeral of aging Laertes, her father-in-law. At night, she undoes her work of the previous day. She never completes the shroud, but now the suitors have found her out. Her trick no longer works.

The situation has become desperate, and every day more so.

TELEMACHUS TAKES ACTION

The action of the epic begins with the goddess Athena appearing in disguise to Telemachus. She advises him to gather an assembly of the island's leaders and, as head of the house, protest the invasion of the suitors. Soon after, he is to visit King Nestor of Pylos and King Menelaus of Sparta, old comrades of Odysseus from the Trojan War, to gather from them any news of his father.

At the assembly, the two leading suitors — Antinous and Eurymachus — confront the prince and his mother. They accuse Penelope of delaying too long in her choice of a new husband. On that acrimonious note, the meeting ends.

Afterwards, as Telemachus secretly sets off for Pylos and Sparta, the suitors plot to assassinate him. At Pylos, Telemachus learns little of his father but is encouraged to visit Sparta. There King Menelaus reports that Odysseus is alive but held captive by the goddess nymph Calypso.

The first four books of the *Odyssey* highlight one of its key themes, the concept of *xenia*, usually translated as *guest-host relationship*. *Xenia* is a reciprocal relationship between two *xenoi* – which means guest, host, stranger, friend, and/or foreigner.

FROM SAVAGERY TO CIVILIZATION

A foreigner can be someone who lives in the next village. Of course, *xenoi* is the word from which we get *xenophobia*, or fear of strangers.

Xenia is not based on friendship. Rather, it's a moral obligation to welcome and protect the stranger. It works only if both sides honor its terms. Failing to honor *xenia* offends Zeus himself, one of whose epithets is *protector of strangers*. Throughout the *Odyssey*, the quality of *xenia* that Odysseus experiences either helps or hinders his attempts to get home and regain his family and kingdom.

TELEMACHUS HONORS XENIA

In the first four books, we witness Telemachus dealing with issues of *xenia* as both host and guest. In a meeting with the goddess Athena, who is disguised as a male guest, Telemachus demonstrates proper *xenia*. It is the first of the *Odyssey's* many host-greeting-guest scenes.

- Telemachus greets his apparently male guest at the door; he relieves him of his spear.

- He bids him welcome, and tells him that his needs will be attended to.

- He offers him food, a bath, and a bed for the night.

- *Only after* Telemachus attends to his guest's immediate physical needs does he ask him who he is.

- Upon leaving the next day, he gives the guest a gift, known as a *guest-gift*.

Remember that Telemachus thinks he's greeting a stranger at the door. They are not friends. They do not know each other. But under the requirements of *xenia*, Telemachus is obligated to welcome the stranger, treat him hospitably, and not delay his departure.

The stranger is likewise obligated to be a good guest – not overstay his welcome, not clean out his host's food supply, not steal the man's wife, and so forth. (*Remember Paris? Unfortunately, we'll always have Paris.*)

XENIA DOUBLY IMPORTANT FOR ODYSSEUS

What's true for Telemachus is doubly true for Odysseus himself. Throughout the epic, he is blown off the map into a world of giants, witches, goddesses and cannibals. The tales of his landfalls and the welcomes he receives differ widely in content and scope.

But the welcomes he receives are all connected by a common theme: **the moral obligation, imposed by supreme Zeus himself upon civilized mankind, to welcome and protect the stranger.**

Whenever Odysseus washes up on a strange shore, he repeats these agonized questions, always spoken in the same way:

… Whose land have I lit on now?
*What **are** they here – violent, savage, lawless? –*
or friendly to strangers, god-fearing men?
— Book VI, Lines 131-133. Robert Fagles translation.

Throughout his voyage, Odysseus depends on the generosity of strangers. Some, such as the Phaeacians and Aeolus, king of the winds, are perfect hosts. They lavishly entertain him and send him on his way with precious gifts. Others are savages, who threaten his life and murder his crew. Still others are overly persistent hostesses who delay their guest's departure.

Consider also the effect of *xenia* beyond the bounds of the *Odyssey*. In the world of the early second millennium BC, no central authority existed to impose law and order. Piracy at sea, cattle raiding and local war by land, and continual bloody competition among rival families were all endemic and unfettered activities. In such a world, a man who left his home was forced to depend on help from strangers. If no universally recognized code of hospitality had existed, few men would have dared travel abroad.

That's why *xenia* became so critical to the economic development of the ancient world, and why the Greeks infused it with so much importance in their mythology. The Greeks invoked Zeus as the divine patron and enforcer of the guest-host code of conduct. Travel, trade and commerce among towns and city-states throughout the region became possible. Civilization more readily spread and indeed flourished.

FROM SAVAGERY TO CIVILIZATION

The observance of *xenia* by guest and host alike became a matter of self-interest to everyone. *Xenia* was especially important to the relatively small and isolated Grecian kingdoms – often separated by sea and mountains. It was less critical, but still important, to the large and populous nations of Persia and Egypt.

WANDERINGS OF ODYSSEUS

Meanwhile, back to the *Odyssey*.

As Books V opens, Homer leaves the story of Telemachus just as the suitors are about to ambush his ship on its return to Ithaca. He now takes up the story of Odysseus as he's about to leave Calypso's island.

At Athena's urging, the gods free Odysseus from Calypso. Odysseus has spent seven years with the goddess. He sleeps with her at night, and pines for his home and family during the day. Calypso is a beautiful, lusty nymph who wants to marry Odysseus and grant him immortality. But he longs for Penelope and the life of a human on Ithaca; he chooses mortality and therefore eventual death. Reluctantly, Calypso sends Odysseus on his way.

Poseidon, the sea god, spots the wayfarer on the open sea. He seeks revenge because Odysseus blinded Poseidon's son, the Cyclops Polyphemus. He shipwrecks Odysseus on Phaeacia, which is ruled by King Alcinous.

The king's daughter, Nausicaa, finds Odysseus washed up on her shore. The Phaeacians are a civilized and hospitable people. They welcome the stranger and encourage him to tell the story of his adventures. Which he does.

Odysseus' narrative is known as *The Wanderings of Odysseus*, fills Books IX-XII, and is the most famous section of the *Odyssey*. His adventures begin at the moment he sails from Troy. It ends years later, when he arrives at Calypso's island. Odysseus narrates the story himself.

At the end of the Trojan War, after some misadventures, Odysseus and his men hope to sail directly home. Instead, a severe storm blows them far off course to the *Land of the Lotus-eaters*. These are not hostile people, but eating the lotus plant removes memory and ambition. Odysseus is barely able to pull his men away and resume the journey.

Moving on, they land on the *Island of the Cyclops*, a race of uncivilized, cannibalistic, one-eyed giants. Curiosity compels Odysseus to explore the island.

One of the giants, Polyphemus, traps Odysseus' scouting party in his cave and eats six of his men. Odysseus escapes by blinding the monster, but in the process incurs the wrath of the giant's father, Poseidon. (We'll come back to this.)

Their next landing is the *Island of Aeolus*, the *wind god*. He is initially a friendly host. He captures all adverse winds and bags them for Odysseus, who is thus able to sail within sight of Ithaca.

Unfortunately, his men suspect that the bag holds treasure. They open it while Odysseus sleeps. The troublesome winds blow the party all the way back to Aeolus, who wants nothing more to do with them. He speculates, correctly, that they must be cursed by the gods.

The next hosts are the cannibalistic *Laestrygonians*. They sink all the ships but Odysseus' own in a surprise attack. The single remaining ship and its crew reach *Aeaea, home of Circe*, a beautiful enchantress. She transforms several of Odysseus' men into pigs. Again Odysseus puts his clever mind to work and defeats Circe. He also becomes her lover. A year later, she lifts the spell from his men and aids in their eventual departure.

However, Circe advises Odysseus that he must first sail to the *Land of the Dead*. While there, he meets with various Greek heroes, visits with his mother, and receives from the seer Tiresias a critical prophecy about his coming trials. Odysseus resumes his journey, and his trials continue. He and his crew barely survive the temptations of the *Sirens' songs* and an attack by a *six-headed monster named Scylla*.

Odysseus and his crew then arrive at the *Island of the Sun God Helios*. Despite severe warnings not to, the men feast on the cattle of the Sun God while Odysseus sleeps. Zeus is outraged and destroys their last ship as the Greeks depart. Everyone except Odysseus is killed.

FROM SAVAGERY TO CIVILIZATION

At last, he is washed ashore at *Calypso's island*, where he stays until released seven years later. Thus ends Odysseus' narration of his adventures after leaving Troy.

ODYSSEUS SLAYS THE SUITORS

When he finishes his story, Odysseus receives the admiration and gifts of the Phaeacians. They follow their tradition of returning wayfaring strangers to their homelands by sailing him to Ithaca.

Odysseus lands on Ithaca, and simultaneously, Athena helps Telemachus avoid the suitors' ambush. She arranges for him to meet his father at their pig farm not far from the palace.

Once on Ithaca, Odysseus promptly prepares to avenge the crimes of his enemies. The suitors are his most formidable enemy, and only he and Telemachus are there to face them. On his previous wanderings, his encounters called upon his resourcefulness, cleverness and judgment in different ways. Those encounters were merely a long prologue to this climactic moment and to this most challenging encounter yet.

Odysseus returns to his home palace disguised as a beggar. He maintains the disguise in front of Penelope, Telemachus, the suitors, the household staff, and his ancient dog Argus. He resists striking back at the suitors who insult and assault him. This hiding of himself is every bit as difficult as his physical trials ever were.

Penelope announces a contest. She vows to wed any man who can string the great bow of Odysseus and shoot an arrow through a dozen axes, as Odysseus once did. Of course, the suitors all fail; only Odysseus himself easily performs this feat.

Then, with help from Athena, Odysseus, Telemachus and two faithful herdsmen slaughter the suitors. The killing of the suitors, their henchmen and disloyal maids is stunning in its brutal, deliberate violence, but it is done in keeping with the requirements of centuries of revenge killing justice. At the end, the house of Odysseus is at last purged of its predators.

Penelope is suspicious that Odysseus is her husband. To assure herself of his identity, Penelope tests him. As he listens, she asks her maid Eurycleia to move the bedstead. King Odysseus himself carved the bed as a young man, built the bedroom around a tree, and knows that the bed cannot be moved. When Odysseus becomes upset that the original bed may have been destroyed, Penelope is relieved and accepts him as her long-absent husband.

Odysseus and Penelope are reunited, as are Odysseus and his aging father, Laertes. Odysseus is home at last.

ODYSSEUS THE EPIC HERO

Odysseus is a different kind of epic hero. He is a warrior – a true Greek hero. He fought and won many battles at Troy. At the same time, he is a model of the worldly, well-traveled, persevering man who overcomes obstacles. He has courage, stamina, and power.

And yet his real strength lies in his intellect, which is shrewd, quick-witted, diplomatic, and resourceful. He is also eloquent and persuasive. Since he lacks supernatural powers or divine heritage, he needs all of these human qualities to survive and make his way home. Both dangers, and temptations to remain in a place, test Odysseus' mettle at every turn. Calypso even offers him immortality, but Odysseus is steadfast in his desire to return home and live the life of a mortal.

In this world of Calypso, as well as Circe, Scylla, and the Sirens, Odysseus is forced to adopt new attitudes and discover new ways of dealing with highly unusual challenges. Odysseus succeeds and in so doing achieves *kleos*, or imperishable fame. He succeeds in part through underhandedness, stealth, and deception. Odysseus is something of a paradox: an epic hero, whose great strength lies in trickery.

Odysseus' name, roughly, means *trouble* in Greek. It refers to both the giving and receiving of trouble. Both kinds occur frequently throughout his wanderings. He demonstrates his heroic trait of cunning intelligence by physically disguising himself, such as appearing as a beggar on Ithaca. And he frequently turns to deceptive speech – many long and meandering but completely convincing lies – to divert attention from the risk of the moment. He tells the Cyclops that his name is *Nobody*. That's perhaps his shortest lie.

Over time, Odysseus learns that to succeed he must at times be cautious and even endure insults in his own home. He proved his valor at Troy by fighting, but in the *Odyssey* he proves his superiority and genius by thinking. Charging bravely ahead with a battle cry is not a recipe for success in the situations Odysseus faces.

FROM SAVAGERY TO CIVILIZATION
ODYSSEUS AND THE CYCLOPS

Perhaps his most famous encounter is with the Cyclops Polyphemus, who kills and eats six of his men. Odysseus must find a way out of the Cyclops' cave before he and the rest of his men are also eaten. Odysseus escapes because of his famous resourcefulness.

But in order to trick the Cyclops, Odysseus must suppress his own identity and give his name as *Nobody*. Of all the hardships with which Odysseus is burdened, of all the challenges he confronts on his wanderings, this challenge, calling himself Nobody, is by far the most difficult. Why is that?

Without doubt, deception is the only possible way out of the Cyclops' cave, the opening of which is plugged. And clearly, Odysseus, as a master of deception, knows precisely what needs to be done. But his whole nature rebels against this particular deception, not telling the Cyclops who he really is. The act of suppressing his identity violates everything he stands for and has done throughout his life.

Expressing his identity – the opposite of suppressing it – is the very reason why he struggles to go on living. He aches to return to the world where the people will know and honor his identity as a mighty Greek hero. He always needs to perpetuate his own imperishable fame and to state his reputation and all that it means.

When he is among the Phaeacians, he reveals his identity at the beginning of his story. He tells the banqueters not only his name but also the renown it carries. He declaims,

> *"I am Odysseus, son of Laertes, known to the world for every kind of craft – my fame has reached the skies."*
> — Book IX, Lines 21-22. Robert Fagles translation.

He speaks of his fame in an utterly objective manner, as if it were something apart from himself. His words are not a boast, but a statement of his reputation, qualities and achievements.

And that is why, once he is free of the Cyclops' cave, he insists, at great risk to himself and his ship, on telling the Cyclops who has blinded him:

THE ODYSSEY BY HOMER

*"Odysseus, raider of cities, **he** gouged out your eye,*
Laertes' son who makes his home in Ithaca!"
— Book IX, Lines 560-562. Robert Fagles translation.

Sailing away from the island of the now zero-eyed Cyclops, he shouts out his name and cries to the heavens that nobody can defeat the *"Great Odysseus!"*

As a practical matter, of course, this was not a good idea. Polyphemus prays to his father, Poseidon. He curses Odysseus, whose real name he now knows. For a very long time thereafter, the enraged Poseidon thwarts Odysseus' homecoming at nearly every turn. But in this incident, still early in his journeys, Odysseus cannot help himself. He must shout out his identity, just as he must also fearlessly bear the cost of his own brashness.

HOMECOMING OF THE EPIC HERO

Throughout his journeys, Odysseus endures pain, suffers deeply, and witnesses much tragedy. He experiences, learns, changes, and grows. At the end of the epic, he finds himself in his most difficult circumstances, about to face the suitors at his palace. He brings to bear all the patience, judgment, and strategic thinking he has gained.

He creates and maintains his physical and verbal disguises. Even when the suitors abuse him, even when he's so close to his wife and son that he can touch them, he quietly endures. Until, just at the right moment, a moment of his choosing, Odysseus reveals his true identity and slays the suitors. And reunites with his also long-suffering wife Penelope.

Odysseus is a champion of heroic intelligence and individual identity. Courage and shrewdness alone once guided him. Now he combines those qualities with the wisdom, judgment and patience steadfastly gained on his adventures.

Odysseus is a true epic hero, and his is a true hero's homecoming.

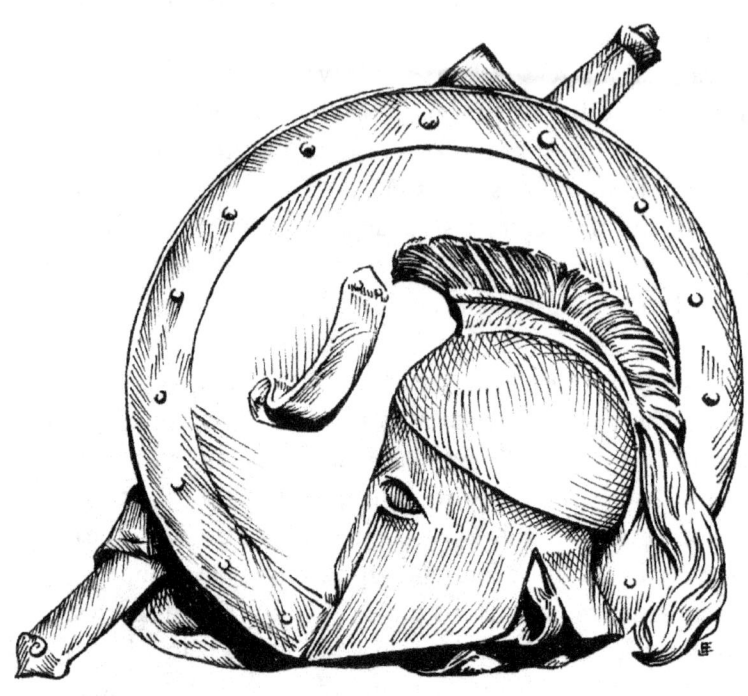

HOMERIC CODE OF HONOR. Homeric heroes pursued KLEOS (imperishable glory) during war. In peacetime or NOSTOS (homecoming, followed by a quiet retirement), they gained kleos through heroic quest. At all times, Homeric heroes lived by the unwritten rules of XENIA (guest-host relationship).

CHAPTER VIII
SYMMETRY OF THE HOMERIC EPICS

AS A WAY OF SUMMING UP THE TROJAN WAR MYTH, I WILL FOCUS ON THE HOMERIC HERO'S CODE OF HONOR, A CODE THAT ORIGINATED WITH THEIR ANCESTORS. We will see how adherence to that code by Homer's characters and their forebears, helped create the overall symmetry that exists between the two epics.

HEROIC PORTRAITS

Homeric heroes pursued *kleos* (imperishable glory) in war and peace. During war, they fearfully balanced in their hearts the allure of *kleos* gained in battle versus *nostos* (homecoming) and a quiet retirement. Whether in war or peace, Homeric heroes tried to live rightly, abiding by the unwritten rules of *kleos, nostos,* and *xenia* (guest-host relationship). Their code reverberated throughout and drove virtually every action and decision in both epics.

Each poem presents a framework of heroic portraits. Achilles serves as the centerpiece in the *Iliad* in pursuit of *kleos*. He represents the warrior's pursuit of immortality through death in battle.

Odysseus, of course, is the centerpiece of the *Odyssey*. In emphasizing his need to return home to Ithaca, Odysseus represents heroic honor code behavior as part of a human's heroic quest during peacetime.

Underlying the actions and decisions of these heroes is *xenia* – the notion of hospitality or the guest-host relationship. To fill the need for social order, *xenia* guided Greek behavior. Through *xenia*, the Greeks understood how to act toward the individual, family, community, assembly of citizens, and indeed even enemies. At all times and in all circumstances, being guided by *xenia* meant living rightly.

BRILLIANT ACHILLES: UNCOMPROMISING MAN

Achilles is a fiercely uncompromising man. He chooses violent death and *kleos* over returning home to a quiet life sans glory. Here is a man of unbending principle who cannot bend his will even just enough to save his own people. Here is a man of constant sorrow, who can never forgive himself for allowing his closest friend, Patroclus, to be killed in his place. Here is a man, finally, of unspeakable anger — anger so intense that Homer used the same word – *menis* – to describe the anger of the gods.

When Patroclus dies, Achilles is consumed by anger. He plumbs the depths of brutality. In a moment of ultimate fury, he boasts that he will eat the flesh of Hector, the man he is about to kill. The *Iliad* is the story of this hero's pain. It culminates in an anger that degrades him to the level of a savage animal.

Until…Until… Until Achilles weeps with King Priam and is moved to render the old man a small kindness. Achilles' savage anger begins to subside. He feels stabs of grief over the loss of Patroclus. Memories of his own father from long ago well up within him. And now, for the first time, Achilles begins to understand that another human being is experiencing an equally painful loss – Priam for the loss of his son Hector.

A moment of self-recognition elevates Achilles from beast to human. He begins to recognize the pain of his deadliest enemy. He also begins to achieve a true recognition of his own humanity. The anger, at least temporarily, abates. And so the story Homer set out to tell in the *Iliad* can end.

Are we surprised by this arc of human experience? We shouldn't be, for we've seen this pattern repeat itself before. We saw it in the myth of Demeter, the goddess who continually suffers, and Persphone, the goddess who repeatedly dies. We saw it in the myth of Dionysus, the suffering and dying and rising god. We saw it in the heroic quest of Heracles. His stupendous crimes led to stupendous suffering, atonement and self-immolation on a funeral pyre. This all-consuming suffering was followed by resurrection and, in the end, immortality.

And we saw this pattern repeat itself in the *Odyssey*.

HEROIC QUEST OF CRAFTY ODYSSEUS

The obvious theme of the *Odyssey* is Odysseus' heroic quest for *nostos*. Thus, it's a *nostos* or peace epic.

Kleos is still very important in the *Odyssey*, still the object of the hero's striving, still the ultimate reason he exists. But now he must achieve *kleos* in a different way. He must follow the more traditional path of a Greek hero's quest, as many of his mythical forebears, such as Theseus and Heracles, had done. Achieving *kleos* in a *nostos* epic does not require the hero to die in battle.

To embark on a heroic quest, the hero must first answer a call to adventure, which for Odysseus is the Trojan War. After the war, he must journey into an outwardly physical unknown and an inwardly psychological unknown. He must encounter many tests and challenges that attempt to throw him off course (Circe, Polyphemus, Sirens, Calypso, et al).

Finally, from a position of rock-bottom (Odysseus names himself *Nobody*, dresses like a beggar) the hero must face his greatest challenge and confront his greatest fear (a hundred suitors). At the end, the hero, having faced death and triumphed, wins back his place of power, with his wife, son and surviving father beside him.

In this way, Odysseus succeeds in fulfilling the requirements of the heroic quest. He achieves *kleos* in peacetime and yet remains alive. Again, unlike Achilles in the *Iliad*, who had to die to achieve *kleos*, Odysseus lives on; indeed, he becomes immortalized. The bards will sing of his exploits in their epic songs for time immemorial (or at least 2500 years), just as they will for Achilles.

CIVILIZATION-ENHANCING XENIA

The civilization-enhancing concept of *xenia* promotes honor code behavior in war and peace. *Xenia* is a moral obligation to welcome and protect the stranger. It is not based on friendship. It works only if each side honors its terms. Failing to honor *xenia* offends Zeus

XENIA in ancient Greece was a sacred reciprocal relationship between two xenoi – which means guest, host, stranger, friend, and/or foreigner. It was a moral obligation to welcome and protect the stranger and worked only if both sides honored its terms.

himself, one of whose epithets is protector of strangers. Examples abound of *xenia* at its best and *xenia* at his worst in both epics:

- The cause of the Trojan War can be traced back to the severe violation of *xenia* by Paris, who abducted Helen.

- King Priam's treatment when he begged Achilles for Hector's body is an example of *xenia* at its best.

- Both Agamemnon and Achilles violated *xenia*. They both refused to accept the honorable offerings of recompense for offenses done to them – Agamemnon when he refused to accept Chryses' offering for the return of his daughter; and Achilles when he refused Agamemnon's offering and admission of wrongdoing.

- Throughout the *Odyssey*, Odysseus' homecoming and the regaining of his family and kingdom are either helped or hindered by the *xenia* he experiences on his journeys. The Phaeacians certainly helped. Polyphemus certainly hindered. The suitors, of course, imposed the greatest hindrance of all.

SYMMETRY OF THE HOMERIC EPICS

Through *kleos, nostos,* and *xenia,* these two monumental compositions – the *Iliad* and the *Odyssey* – balance each other out. They offer a steady rhythmic flow of dactylic hexameters (or iambic pentameter in English translations) throughout their vast stretches of narrative. The *Iliad* contains more than 15,000 lines; the *Odyssey,* more than 12,000.

The balancing allows the reader to focus on the central plot and characterization of the principal hero in each. Achilles, the mightiest and least compromising warrior, is hugely proud of his martial exploits and physical prowess. He is matched against the many-sidedness of Odysseus, famed for his crafty stratagems and cunning intelligence.

SYMMETRY OF THE HOMERIC EPICS

The symmetry of the *Iliad* and *Odyssey* goes further. Between them, the two epics incorporate most of whatever was worth retelling about the Heroic Age - at least from the standpoint of a fifth century BC Greek.

The *Iliad* tells the story that it says it will tell — about Achilles' anger and how it led to countless woes. It also retells, or even relives, directly or indirectly, the entire tale of Troy, including the judgment of Paris, the abduction of Helen, the sacrifice of Iphigenia, and the foreshadowing of the death of Achilles.

In short, although the *Iliad* directly covers only a short stretch of the whole story of Troy, it still says something about practically everything that happened there. The *Odyssey* adds much more, including the Trojan horse deception and the sack of Troy.

HOMER AND HESIOD ABIDE

The fifth century BC Greeks thought of Homer and Hesiod as their first authors, their primary authors. The work of those two represents the foundation and earliest phase of Greek literature.

The father of history himself, Herodotus, observed in his *Histories* that Homer and Hesiod, by way of their songs, gave the Greeks their first definitive statement about the gods, in effect defining their own society. This observation by Herodotus claimed that the songs of Homer and Hesiod are the basis of Greek civilization.

HOMERIC CODE OF HONOR

We should have a sense now of how that began.

Millennia ago, near the very beginning, Prometheus created man to stand erect and look like the gods, stole fire for man, and taught him to outwit the gods. From that moment, the Greeks began developing, and orally transmitting down the centuries, an ancient code of behavior.

Under the code, men knew how to live rightly – both in frequent times of war and rare moments of peace. The code of behavior was their orally transmitted guidebook, becoming ever more sophisticated and comprehensive as the centuries passed. It reached its apotheosis as the heroic code of honor demonstrated in the Homeric epics. By developing, adhering to, and passing along this code, the ancient Greeks stumbled their way toward a more civilized world. It was an exceedingly hard journey, but it had a stupendous outcome, the likes of which leave the world agape still today.

The gold funerary MASK OF AGAMEMNON, dubbed the Mona Lisa of Prehistory. German archaeologist Heinrich Schliemann discovered it at Mycenae in 1876. He believed it to be the body of King Agamemnon, leader of the Greeks during the Trojan War (1194-1184 BC), as described in Homer's Iliad. However, the mask probably predates the Trojan War by about 300 years.

CHAPTER IX
MYTH OF THE HOUSE OF ATREUS
THE ORESTEIA BY AESCHYLUS: AGAMEMNON, LIBATION BEARERS, AND EUMENIDES

IN APRIL 1968, SENATOR ROBERT F. KENNEDY, WHO WAS RUNNING FOR PRESIDENT, MADE A ROUTINE CAMPAIGN STOP AT A POOR BLACK NEIGHBORHOOD IN INDIANAPOLIS. He had learned on his way there that Martin Luther King, Jr., had just been assassinated. The crowd didn't have this information yet, so the New York senator had to announce the dreadful news.

Kennedy struggled to find appropriate language for the day's tragedy. And, of course, this murder would have recalled to everyone's mind the assassination of his brother John five years earlier.

In the end, Sen. Kennedy turned to the *Oresteia* of Aeschylus – as Bernard Knox calls it, *"The grand trilogy from ancient Greece about the search for justice in a world filled with continually erupting and pervasive violence."*

When Kennedy stood before the crowd, he quoted these lines, in which the chorus of city elders ponders the meaning of violence and suffering:

Even in our sleep, pain which cannot forget
falls drop by drop upon the heart,
until, in our own despair,
against our will,
comes wisdom
through the awful grace of God.
— The Greek Way, 1930. Translated by Edith Hamilton.

Kennedy concluded his remarks by exhorting his audience to heed the wisdom of the ancient classics: *"Let us dedicate ourselves to what the Greeks wrote so many years ago: to tame the savageness of man and make gentle the life of this world."*

Of course, just three months later, when Kennedy himself was murdered, it became achingly clear that the savageness of man would not be tamed any time soon. Those lines of Aeschylus that Kennedy cited on the night of King's death became the epitaph on his own tombstone.

FROM SAVAGERY TO CIVILIZATION

Kennedy's call to heed the words of the *Oresteia* has never been more existentially relevant to humanity than it is today. The success of that effort has, perhaps, never seemed so far out of reach. Let's examine the trilogy in the context of its mythic background.

TRILOGY ABOUT A FAMILY CURSE

The walled city of Mycenae was the family home of the House of Atreus around 1100 BC. It sits toward the northeast corner of the Peloponnesus in Greece. The surrounding area, including the nearby town Argos, was all part of Agamemnon's kingdom. I'm told that stains of blackened blood still mark that unhappy place.

Tantalus was the founder of the House of Atreus. He had one son Pelops. Pelops had two sons: Thyestes and Atreus. Atreus begot two sons. One, Menelaus, became the king of Sparta and made Helen his queen. The other, Agamemnon, ruled over Mycenae with his wife Clytemnestra and their four children: Iphigenia, Electra, Orestes, and Chrysomethis.

The *Oresteia* is a trilogy about the family curse that doomed the House of Atreus. The three plays of the trilogy are the *Agamemnon*, *The Libation Bearers (Women Carrying Libations)*, and *Eumenides (Kindly Ones)*.

CURSE OF THE HOUSE OF ATREUS

In the trilogy, Aeschylus laid bare the myth of the cursed House of Atreus, the families of Agamemnon and Menelaus. He offered his vision of that curse being carried to its conclusion.

Aeschylus also used the story of the House of Atreus to explore issues of justice, revenge, and individual responsibility. He reshaped the traditional myth to his own purposes. He celebrated man's capacity for suffering. He shed light on the formation of the Athenian court system by dramatizing the ancient issue of personal vendetta versus social litigation.

TROJAN WAR MYTH

We already know how closely interwoven the myth of the House of Atreus is with the Trojan War. It marked the end of the Heroic Age and the beginning of purely human history. The Trojan War was the last episode in which the great heroes of myth, who were somehow closer to the gods than normal human beings, took part in recorded events.

To Greeks of the Classical Age, the heroes of the Trojan War were the ancestors of families alive in their own time. Thus, when Aeschylus staged the *Oresteia* in 458 BC, he could assume that his audience thoroughly knew the Trojan War story as well as all the other subsidiary stories interwoven with it, including the myth of the House of Atreus.

To those audiences, these stories were their own history, not simply myths reenacted on a stage. For them, Trojan War events actually occurred, and the ancestors of fifth century BC Athenians had taken part in them – those many hundreds of years earlier. The Greeks also believed the stories surrounding the House of Atreus, all the way back to their horrid beginnings.

HEREDITARY CURSE OF THE HOUSE OF ATREUS

The House of Atreus was the embodiment of savagery, the archetypal dysfunctional family. No other Greek family could rival it for accumulated atrocities. Multigenerational stories of murder, rape, incest, adultery and cannibalism, *just within the family*, are repeated over and over again. Their hereditary curse repeats itself, works itself out, and repeats itself again, generation after generation.

The concept of a hereditary curse is that moral guilt can be inherited. If someone dies with a great deal of moral guilt, his heirs will inherit that guilt. The sins of the fathers are passed on to their children, whether they like it or not.

In the case of the House of Atreus, the hereditary curse manifests itself through, and is caused by, excessive intergenerational violence. In this family, parents kill children; children kill parents; and strong servings of adultery, rape, incest, and cannibalism keep things spicy.

TANTALUS' BANQUET CRIME

The curse began, not with Agamemnon, not with Agamemnon's father Atreus, not with Agamemnon's grandfather Pelops, but with Tantalus, Agamemnon's great-grandfather and founder of the family line.

In the most commonly related version of the story, Tantalus offends the gods by trying to trick them into eating the flesh of Pelops, his son. Tantalus kills Pelops, chops him into pieces, cooks those in a stew, and offers his son's flesh to the gods at a banquet. Apparently, Tantalus is trying to show that the gods are not so superior to human beings. They can be tricked into eating a human child's flesh.

But his trick doesn't work. The gods are not fooled into committing a crime.

(*It actually wasn't that hard to figure out. It said Pelops Special right on the menu, nine drachmas. Baby-backed ribs also available, two drachmas*).

The gods realize perfectly well who Pelops is and refrain from eating him. Instead, they restore the boy to his former self.

(*Demeter, goddess of grain and agriculture, receives word too late that she isn't supposed to eat the stew. So she accidentally eats Pelops' shoulder. To remedy the loss of the boy's shoulder, the gods reshape a piece of marble. They create a new shoulder for the boy – the first artificial limb transplant.*)

This was the family's first crime. The founder murdered his own child and tempted the gods with cannibalism.

The gods curse Tantalus and condemn him to starve in the underworld, tormented by eternal hunger and thirst. He stands forever in a pool; the water comes up to his chin. Fruit trees grow along the shore; he can almost touch them. Whenever he tries to eat the fruit, the wind blows it just out of reach. Whenever he stoops to drink the water, it flows away. And so Tantalus is eternally tantalized by what he desires but cannot have.

PELOPS' CHILDREN UNDER DOUBLE CURSE

Pelops, too, when he grows up, incurs a curse upon himself and upon his descendants. However, Pelops differs from his family. First, he does not direct his violent actions against a member of his own family. Rather, he murders his future father-in-law and that father-in-law's charioteer, a slave named Myrtilos. Second, Pelops, once his body is fully restored, does not himself suffer the ill effects of the family curse.

Pelops incurs a curse on himself and, more importantly, on his descendants because of his actions when he decides to marry a woman named Hippodameia. Hippodameia's father has decreed that, in order to marry her, a suitor must defeat him, her father, in a chariot race. If the suitor fails to win the chariot race, he will be killed.

Pelops wants to marry Hippodameia, but he doesn't want to die. He decides to win her hand by cheating. He bribes Myrtilos to remove the linchpins from the king's chariot and replace them with wax. This Myrtilos does. As a result, the king's chariot crashes, and he is killed. Myrtilos flees the city with Pelops and Hippodameia. That first night out, Myrtilos tries to have sex with Hippodameia. Pelops kills him by throwing him over a cliff.

Those are Pelops' two acts of violence: first, killing Hippodameia's father, then killing Myrtilos. As Myrtilos falls to his death, he screams out a curse against Pelops and all of his descendants forever. Thus, by the time Pelops' children are born, they already suffer under the weight of a double curse. They inherit the family guilt incurred by their grandfather Tantalus, and, as Pelops' children, they are directly cursed by Myrtilos.

ATREUS AND THYESTES AT A FAMILY BANQUET

When Pelops dies, his two sons, Atreus and Thyestes, quarrel over the kingship of Mycenae. Finally, they agree, at Thyestes' suggestion, that the brother who owns a particular fleece of a particular golden lamb should be king. Atreus has such a fleece, so he agrees. However, Thyestes has seduced Atreus' wife, Aerope, and she has given him the fleece. With that maneuver, Thyestes tries to claim the throne, but his trickery is soon discovered. Thyestes is banished, and Atreus becomes king.

However, Atreus seeks revenge because Thyestes has seduced his wife. So he invites Thyestes back to Mycenae to reconcile their differences and celebrate their reconciliation. He tells Thyestes to bring his children.

When Thyestes reaches Mycenae, Atreus hosts a celebratory banquet. And guess what they have for dinner. Atreus has killed and cooked Thyestes' sons. He serves them to their father as a dish at the banquet. Thyestes has no idea he is eating the flesh of his own sons. After he eats, Atreus presents him with a platter; on it are the two boys' little hands and feet.

THYESTES SEEKS REVENGE

Thyestes curses Atreus and his descendants and goes back into banishment. On the advice of an oracle while in exile, Thyestes fathers a son, Aegisthus, on his own daughter, so that he has someone to avenge the wrongs done to him. So now incest enters the picture. Aegisthus will play a crucial role as the family curse further unravels.

Atreus incurs a curse on himself through his actions. He is also directly cursed by his brother Thyestes. Once again, we have a man killing male children of his own bloodline. We have an elder generation male killing males of the next generation, and doing so in order to force an unwitting victim in his bloodline into cannibalism.

Atreus and Thyestes bring together several lines of hideousness. First we have basic cannibalism, which is awful enough. But that is followed by the shriek-inducing cannibalism of a father eating his own children. The murder count rises. Rape, incest, adultery, and incestuous rape, all contribute to the character smear.

TRIPLE GENERATIONAL CURSE

We now come to the present generation of the House of Atreus – King Agamemnon and Clytemnestra of Mycenae with their children Iphigenia, Electra, Orestes, and Chrysomethis; King Menelaus and Helen of Sparta; and their cousin Aegisthus. All of the darkest elements of the family's triple generational curse now coalesce.

As with previous generations, these characters are doomed to reiterate and reenact the same pattern of the family curse. Although Menelaus seems largely to escape this fate, Agamemnon suffers the full brunt of this disastrous curse in his own life.

SACRIFICE OF IPHIGENIA

Before Helen married Menelaus, most of the Greek chieftains in the region sought her as a mate, for, as we have learned, she is the most beautiful woman in the world. The chieftains also made a pact.

They would accept without protest her choice of a husband and come to his aid if anyone attempted to steal her from him.

As we know, that's exactly what happens. Paris seduces Helen and carries her back to Troy. Faithful to their oaths, the chieftains mobilize a great force to capture Troy and restore Helen to Menelaus, her rightful husband. Agamemnon, as leader of the largest contingent and as Menelaus' older brother, becomes commander of the entire fleet.

The expedition assembles at Aulis, on the eastern coast of Greece, but is unable to sail for Troy because of adverse winds. You've heard this before. Calchas, a soothsayer who accompanies the army, declares that the goddess Artemis is responsible for the lack of favorable winds. She can only be appeased by the sacrifice of Agamemnon's daughter, Iphigenia.

For the sake of his army, Agamemnon agrees. He induces Clytemnestra to bring Iphigenia to Aulis. When the young girl arrives at the camp, Agamemnon sacrifices her to the goddess Artemis in place of a sacrificial animal – one more family killing. After that, the wind changes, and the army sets sail for Troy.

AEGISTHUS RETURNS TO ARGOS

While Agamemnon fights in the Trojan War, Aegisthus returns to Argos. He plots against his cousin. He means to regain his rightful place on the throne of Mycenae. He also wants to avenge the treatment of his father and brothers at the hands of Atreus.

At the same time, Clytemnestra has come to bitterly hate Agamemnon for sacrificing their daughter – a hatred that grows and festers. She and Aegisthus conspire together. They become lovers, or perhaps just passionate co-haters. The pair hatches a plan to murder Agamemnon when he returns from Troy.

The siege of Troy lasts ten years. Finally the city falls and is sacked by the Greek army. Greek warriors destroy Trojan temples and sell surviving inhabitants into slavery. A case of blood vengeance through genocide.

FROM SAVAGERY TO CIVILIZATION
JUSTICE THROUGH REVENGE

The plot of the *Oresteia* depends entirely on the theme of revenge and retaliation. Revenge motivates the actions of almost all of the characters, and causes almost all of the effects within the play. The effects take a slippery slope form. Retaliation by one character begets a revenge killing, which in turn begets more retaliation — rinse and repeat, generation after generation. We've already seen what earlier members of the family — Tantalus, Pelops, Atreus and Thyestes — contributed to this curse.

Now, with that mythic background as context, the *Oresteia* opens. The action of the trilogy concerns itself with the murder of Agamemnon by his wife Clytemnestra, the murder of Clytemnestra and Aegisthus by Orestes, the trial of Orestes, the lifting of the curse on the House of Atreus, and the pacification of the Furies.

AS THE ORESTEIA OPENS...

It all begins in the *Agamemnon*. We are now in the middle of the next generation, whose turn it is to perpetuate the curse. The pace of revenge killing is about to quicken once again.

In the major event of the play, Clytemnestra murders Agamemnon with several hacks of an ax in his bath. She avenges the death of their daughter Iphigenia at his hands. She also murders Agamemnon's concubine, Cassandra, daughter of King Priam of Troy, thus also avenging her husband's philandering. Aegisthus stands by to aid and abet.

Later, in *The Libation Bearers*, Orestes and Electra, children of Agamemnon and Clytemnestra, plot to carry the curse to the next generation. To avenge their father's murder by their mother, Orestes, pressured by Electra, murders Clytemnestra and her lover Aegisthus – a case of matricide plus garden-variety homicide, but still all in the family.

In the third play, *Eumenides*, the Furies hunt down Orestes to wreak judgment on him for his crime of matricide. The Furies take vengeance on those who have harmed blood relatives, especially children who have harmed their parents. Even Clytemnestra's spirit urges the Furies on. She demands that they kill Orestes and wreak vengeance on her behalf.

Although Orestes willingly admits he has committed murder, he does not himself know whether he has done right or wrong. Finally, the goddess Athena intervenes and calms the Furies. After the blood of generations has been spilt, the cycle of non-stop retaliation and revenge comes to an end.

JUSTICE THROUGH LAW

Athena introduces a new legal system – a special court – for meting out justice. This replaces the ancient retributive law of retaliation. The special court is to decide the guilt or innocence of Orestes. However, the jurors are unable to reach a verdict, so Athena casts the deciding vote. Orestes is acquitted.

Thus, the Furies, demons of primitive vendetta law, are prevented from killing Orestes and committing one more act of blood vengeance. The cycle of revenge is broken. But upon hearing the innocent verdict, the Furies angrily threaten vengeance (again).

But Athena calms the Furies by offering them a position of honor in her city. They accept. The ancient Furies are thus transformed into benevolent spirits in Athens. Their name is changed to the Eumenides, or Kindly Ones, to symbolize their new character.

BLUEPRINT FOR HANDLING FUTURE REVENGE KILLINGS

The action in *Eumenides* marks a shift in the justice theme – from justice through revenge and retaliation, to justice through the law. Orestes begs Athena for deliverance from the Fates. She grants his request in an unprecedented way.

Athena does not simply forgive Orestes and forbid the Furies from chasing him. She puts him on trial to find a just answer to the question of his guilt or innocence in the murder of Clytemnestra. This is the first example of proper litigation. It illuminates the change that has just occurred. The cultural response of thousands of years is to retaliate and avenge an alleged crime. Not this time. This time, Athena pushes the culture to civilized decision-making.

Instead of allowing the Furies to torture Orestes, she forces both the Furies and Orestes to plead their case before she renders a verdict. In addition, so that everything is dealt with fairly, Athena sets up the ground rules for how the verdict will be decided.

Athena creates a blueprint for handling future revenge-killings. The blueprint might eventually help eliminate merciless hunting by the Furies. Once the trial concludes, Athena proclaims Orestes' innocence, and he is set free. The cycle of murder and revenge has been broken; the foundation for future litigation has been laid.

(*Lawyers everywhere rejoiced. And law schools sprouted up across the land like grass after a spring rain.*)

Establishing the rule of law means institutionalizing justice. Justice is no longer a personal responsibility to be meted out according to the rule of family vendetta. It is now a state responsibility embodied in the law. The state, representing the community as a whole, has established that law. This is a major step forward.

MAN'S STUMBLING PROGRESS

Of course, there were efforts before those of Aeschylus to map out mankind's stumbling progress. The parables of Hesiod and Homer marked the gradually higher levels of social existence the early Greeks achieved.

Notably, Hesiod in his *Theogony* traced the original gods themselves from savagery to, if not civilization, then to a peak of absolute control. Zeus ruled on high because he was too strong for the law of retaliation that consumed his forebears. He was the invincible masculine will, the way of might makes right.

The action of Homer's epics occurred thousands of years later. Over that period from the beginning, mankind developed a code to guide him in right and orderly behavior. The code was their social relations guidebook, unwritten but universally understood.

The code became more sophisticated and comprehensive as the generations passed, and culminated in Homer's heroic code of honor. It governed how a man conducts himself in battle during wartime, and interacts with his family and community at all times.

But despite the progress made throughout those centuries, there remained only one effective way to achieve social justice. The notion of individual revenge killing to achieve social justice reigned supreme, and worked exceedingly well for thousands of years.

Gradually, however, the process deteriorated – from the pure to the problematic. Acts of recklessness and blood vengeance seemed to go on forever. Proper honor code behavior collapsed into the brute force of individual vengeance. Men cursed offenders and their heirs' offenders; their heirs were then cursed with endless acts of violence.

From the beginning, individual revenge killings were the punishments of the Furies. They represented real, objective law – blood will have blood. But in the end their system – justice by revenge and retaliation – belonged to a barbaric, not a civilized, society.

RITES OF PASSAGE

In order to reach a higher plane of civilization, the Greek people — from individual heroes to tribes to the entire culture — had to, by necessity, undergo rites of passage. Through these, the culture shifted over time — from achieving justice through tribal blood vendettas, to ensuring justice through a system of civilized social decision-making.

The *Oresteia* shows us how that happened, and how its achievement revolutionized the ancient world. The works of Homer and Hesiod, and myths about ancient Greek heroes, provide evidence of tribal rites of passage. Each contribution helped carry the culture step by step out of barbarism. The trilogy of Aeschylus is the culmination of those contributions.

This was the process of a rite of passage – a painful initiation, suffering and death (or symbolic death), followed by atonement and redemption to a higher plane. This was the common tribal rite of passage in the making of an ancient Greek hero.

Recall the myth of Heracles. He passed through fire – suffering, pain and the real death of his body. It was necessary for him, a mortal human being, to suffer in that way in order to become immortal.

Recall the myth of Dionysus. He was already a god but was forced to suffer extreme pain, having his body ripped apart, in order for his divinity to be accepted. And recall Homer's epic heroes (Achilles, Odysseus, et al.) who each passed through their own rites of passage from suffering and pain to death, to redemption.

Remember the words of Aeschylus:
> *Even in our sleep, pain which cannot forget*
> *falls drop by drop upon the heart,*

until, in our own despair,
against our will,
comes wisdom
through the awful grace of God.

The *Oresteia* is the representation of that rite of passage that the Greek culture itself underwent.

THE ORESTEIA - CULTURAL RITE OF PASSAGE

First, the king had to die. The *Agamemnon* is the rite of separation. The king is cut off from his society. Suffering, pain and death follow for the members of the already long-suffering House of Atreus.

The Libation Bearers comes next. It's a rite of transition. The son, Orestes, arrives at the threshold of maturity.

And finally, the *Eumenides* offers us the rite of aggregation. It brings the family together. Atonement is complete. The curse is lifted.

The family celebrates Orestes' initiation as the new king. We will never hear much about him again. The family will now become normal, average, perhaps anonymous. They have played their part. But overall Greek culture will now function at a higher, more civilized level, as seen by the audience's initiation into fifth century BC Athenian justice.

The *Oresteia*, finally, represents the Greek culture's rite of passage from savagery to civilization.

CHAPTER X
MYTH OF THE HOUSE OF OEDIPUS
SOPHOCLES' TRAGEDIES: OEDIPUS THE KING, OEDIPUS AT COLONUS, AND ANTIGONE

OEDIPUS THE KING

AMONG THE APPROXIMATELY 200 GREEK TRAGEDIES THAT HAVE SURVIVED UNTIL TODAY, ONLY ONE TRUE TRILOGY EXISTS — THE ORESTEIA BY AESCHYLUS. It consists of three plays written in chronological order with a single narrative thread.

The Oedipus plays of Sophocles, sometimes called the Oedipus trilogy or the Theban trilogy, are not a trilogy. Sophocles' three plays were not written or staged at the same time. *Antigone* was probably staged around 442 BC; *Oedipus the King* – 13 years later, about 429; and *Oedipus at Colonus* probably in 401, five years after Sophocles died and some 40 years after he wrote *Antigone*.

BLIND OEDIPUS wandered for many years in exile, banished from Thebes because of his sin. He was an abject beggar, a wreck of a man. Blind and frail, he walked with the help of his daughter Antigone.

We will not discuss these plays in the order in which they were written, but rather in the order of Sophocles' overall storyline – *Oedipus the King, Oedipus at Colonus,* and *Antigone.* We'll also treat them as three distinct plays that happen to contain the same major characters. Since the three do not express a single narrative thread, the actions of the players are sometimes inconsistent from play to play.

PATTERN OF SOPHOCLEAN TRAGIC HERO

Sophocles' plays are different in another way from the trilogy of Aeschylus. More so than Aeschylus, Sophocles concentrates his attention on an individual. The protagonist is isolated, apart, alone, and facing a terrible struggle or problem.

One critic, Bernard Knox, said that Sophocles invented the tragic hero, that is, the hero as main character of a tragedy, to describe the protagonists of his plays. Oedipus is the kind of tragic hero we see later in *Hamlet* and is of a different sort than the heroes found in Homeric epics.

These three plays, like most of Sophocles' extant plays, take their names from their main characters – Oedipus and Antigone. Although the circumstances differ, they fit the same basic pattern.

The protagonist is faced with a crisis. He or she can only avert disaster by agreeing to a compromise that would betray something he or she holds to be supremely important. The protagonist refuses to compromise, despite persuasive speeches, threats, or violence – or all three. The protagonist remains steadfast in his or her refusal to compromise. The end result is his or her destruction.

Other characters, or the chorus, refer to the protagonists of these plays as being *deinos*. *Deinos* is an ambiguous Greek word meaning – all at once – wondrous and awe-inspiring, terrible and frightening, or just simply strange. A *deinos* protagonist is frequently set alongside another character who is more like a normal human being. That brings out their implacable nature and essential oddity by comparison. These characters are not cuddly, friendly, affectionate people. Rather, they are both repellent and admirable.

Another noteworthy characteristic, typical of Sophoclean tragedy, is that the gods do not appear in the Oedipus plays. Instead, the characters must determine the will of the gods by interpreting inherently ambiguous omens and prophecies. This lack of help from the gods underscores the isolation of the Sophoclean hero. He cannot turn to the gods for help.

Let's turn now to Sophocles' *Oedipus the King*.

MYTH OF OEDIPUS THE KING

In the basic myth, Oedipus is the baby son of Laius and Jocasta, king and queen of Thebes. An oracle has told them that Jocasta's forthcoming son will grow up to kill his father and marry his mother. To prevent that terrible fate, Laius and Jocasta leave the baby out in the countryside to die shortly after he is born (this was an acceptable practice in that time and place). However, the infant is rescued and brought up by someone else. He doesn't know who his true parents are and thus grows up unaware of his true identity.

In the next part of the myth, the now grown infant, who has been named Oedipus by his adoptive parents, returns to his native town of Thebes. These days, a part-human, part-animal monster named the Sphinx has been terrorizing the citizens of Thebes. She requires each person to answer a riddle. If they cannot answer the riddle, she kills them. Oedipus overcomes the Sphinx by answering her riddle.

The people of Thebes are grateful to Oedipus for freeing them from the Sphinx, and so they make him their king. He replaces their old king, Laius, who has recently been killed. In addition to awarding the kingship of Thebes to Oedipus, the Thebans also offer him the hand of the queen of Thebes in marriage. The queen of Thebes, of course, is none other than Jocasta, his real mother, although nobody knows it, least of all Oedipus.

In the last part of the myth, Oedipus rules Thebes for several years. He is ignorant of what he has done. He and Jocasta have four children. The whole truth is not discovered until after these children are born. The old king, Laius, died because Oedipus killed him without knowing who he was. And now Oedipus is married to, and has had children with, his own mother. When the truth finally comes out, Jocasta kills herself. Oedipus immediately blinds himself and goes into exile from Thebes.

FROM SAVAGERY TO CIVILIZATION
SOPHOCLES ADDS DETAILS TO THE MYTHS

That is the basic myth of Oedipus. However, Sophocles added a few telling details of his own. First, in the Sophoclean version, Jocasta gives the infant Oedipus to a trusted slave, a shepherd, and asks the slave to abandon the baby in the wilderness.

But, instead of leaving the baby on the ground to die, the shepherd hands the baby over to a Corinthian shepherd who pastures his flocks on the same mountain. The Corinthian shepherd knows that the king and queen of Corinth, Polybus and Merope, are childless, and so he takes the baby to them. Oedipus is thus raised as a prince of Corinth, and believes that Polybus and Merope are his true parents.

Here's another detail added by Sophocles. When Oedipus becomes a young man, a guest at a banquet taunts him by saying, *"You are not really Polybus' son; nobody knows who you are."*

This greatly disturbs Oedipus. So he travels to Apollo's Oracle at Delphi and asks, *"Am I the son of Polybus and Merope?"*

But the Oracle does not answer the question. The Oracle says only, *"You will kill your father and marry your mother."*
Oedipus promptly leaves Corinth, never to return, in order to avoid killing his parents. Oedipus heads toward Thebes.

On the road to Thebes, Oedipus meets, quarrels with, and kills an old man at a crossroads. The old man happens to be Laius, his true father, although Oedipus does not learn this until much later.

When Oedipus arrives in Thebes, he discovers that the Theban King Laius has been recently killed. However, the one eyewitness to Laius' murder swears that Laius was killed by a band of robbers. And so no one, neither Oedipus nor anyone else, immediately connects the old man Oedipus has killed and King Laius, who has been killed by a band of robbers. Because Laius is dead, and because Oedipus has solved the riddle of the Sphinx, he is given the kingship of Thebes and Jocasta's hand in marriage.

In the play, the truth of what actually has happened, and who Oedipus actually is, emerges in fragmented, non-chronological order. Oedipus violates two of the most formidable taboos of almost every human society. But Sophocles does not focus specifically on those actions – neither the murder of Oedipus' father Laius, nor the incest with his mother Jocasta.

Instead, Sophocles focuses on the moment Oedipus discovers the truth. This discovery occurs neither by divine intervention nor by chance. Rather, Oedipus' determination to know his own origins combines with his own persistent, courageous actions to lead to his discovery of the truth. The hero of the play is thus his own destroyer. He is the detective who tracks down and identifies the criminal – who turns out to be himself.

AS OEDIPUS THE KING OPENS...

With that as mythic background, let's turn to the play itself. As it opens, Oedipus is in his full regal role as head of state, dedicated to the interests and needs of Thebes. He enforces the law. He investigates, prosecutes, and judges criminals. In all these respects, Oedipus personifies triumphant human progress — from primitive barbarism to the highest civilization of the city-state – the notion first introduced in the *Oresteia* of Aeschylus.

The play begins with the words of a priest, who is accompanied by the chorus of Theban citizens. They beg Oedipus to find a cure for a terrible plague that ravages the city. Oedipus has already sent his brother-in-law Creon to learn the cause of the plague from the Delphic Oracle. Creon returns and reports that pollution is on the land because the murderer of Laius is still living, unknown, in Thebes. Oedipus responds by invoking a solemn, formal curse against the murderer of Laius. He says:

> *I order you, every citizen of the state*
> *where I hold throne and power: banish this man –*
> *whoever he may be – never shelter him, never*
> *speak a word to him, never make him partner*
> *to your prayers, your victims burned to the gods....*
> *He is the plague, the heart of our corruption....*

And then he finishes:

> *I curse myself as well... if by any chance*
> *he proves to be an intimate of our house,*
> *here at my hearth, with my full knowledge,*
> *may the curse I just called down on him strike me!*
>
> — *Oedipus the King,* Lines 269-287. Robert Fagles translation.

This is the first of many highly ironic speeches by Oedipus. He just cursed himself without knowing that he cursed himself. He also clearly and accurately states his own position – he is the plague and corruptor of his own land.

"YOU ARE THE LAND'S POLLUTION" — TIRESIAS

He then summons the seer Tiresias to identify the murderer. Tiresias is obviously reluctant to do so. This arouses Oedipus' anger and suspicion. He thinks the seer is being unhelpful because he cares nothing about Thebes. Or maybe, he thinks, Tiresias helped plot the murder of Laius.

Oedipus' anger enrages Tiresias in turn. The prophet tells Oedipus, *"You are the land's pollution."*

Oedipus now thinks Tiresias is simply trying to taunt and slander him, because he knows that he cannot be Laius' murderer. Laius was murdered by many men, not by one.

Oedipus next directly accuses Creon of treachery. Then Jocasta steps forward to help calm Oedipus and ease the quarrel. Jocasta says, in part, that oracles can safely be disregarded, and that we don't need to pay attention to this one. As she speaks, she mentions a crucial piece of information that no one had disclosed or heard before. She says:

> *An oracle came to Laius one fine day ...and it declared*
> *that doom would strike him down at the hands of a son,*
> *our son, to be born of our own flesh and blood. But Laius,*
> *so the report goes at least, was killed by strangers,*
> *thieves, at a place where three roads meet... my son —*
> *he wasn't three days old and the boy's father*
> *fastened his ankles, had a henchman fling him away*
> *on a barren, trackless mountain....*
> *Apollo brought neither thing to pass...*
> *That's how the seers and all their revelations*
> *mapped out the future. Brush them from your mind.*
> — *Oedipus the King,* Lines 784-800. Robert Fagles translation.

The one crucial bit of information that Jocasta let slip, the one thing no one has ever said to Oedipus before, is that Laius was killed at a place where three roads meet. Oedipus knows that he killed an old man right before he came to Thebes, at a place where three roads meet.

To Jocasta's story, Oedipus reacts with absolute horror. Speaking of the man he killed he says:

> *Oh, but if there is any blood-tie*
> *between Laius and this stranger...*
> *what man alive more miserable than I?*
> *More hated by the gods? I am the man...*
> *And all these curses I – no one but I*
> *brought down these piling curses on myself!...*
> *Wasn't I born for torment? Look me in the eyes!*
> *I am abomination – heart and soul!*
>   — *Oedipus the King*, Lines 899-911. Robert Fagles translation.

At this point, Oedipus suspects only that the old man he killed might have been Laius. He has no inkling yet of the full horror that awaits him, and so he persists in learning the truth, whatever it may be.

OEDIPUS QUESTIONS EYEWITNESSES

Oedipus sends for the witness to Laius' death, to question him. While we wait for him to arrive, a messenger comes from Corinth to tell Oedipus that Polybus is dead. Oedipus reacts not with grief but with joy, and declares that Apollo's oracle was false. The messenger is astonished and puzzled by Oedipus' reaction to the news. Thinking to comfort his new king, the messenger tells Oedipus that he is not the true son of Polybus and Merope. The messenger knows this for a fact, because he is the one who gave the baby to the Corinthian king and queen.

When Oedipus asks him who gave him the baby, it turns out that the slave who has already been summoned, the witness to Laius' death, is the same Theban shepherd who handed the baby over. At this point, Oedipus' entire focus changes. It's no longer a question of, "*Who killed Laius?*" Oedipus' question now is, "*Who am I?*"

Jocasta realizes who Oedipus is before he does. She desperately tries to stop him from asking more questions. She tells him, "*Just leave it alone. What does it matter who you are? Just stop right here.*"

But Oedipus' search will not be turned away. Jocasta rushes inside the building, leaving Oedipus to wait for the old Theban slave.

When the slave arrives, the encounter between these two characters brings together all the threads of the story. Finally, Oedipus recognizes the truth. These two men, the Theban slave and the Corinthian slave, are the two eyewitnesses to the defining moments of Oedipus' life – the trade-off when Oedipus was an infant, and the deaths of both of Oedipus' fathers. When Oedipus melds their two stories together, the complete picture of who he actually is emerges.

TRAGIC DOWNFALL OF KING OEDIPUS

Oedipus recognizes his own identity. He also recognizes that the prophecies given to his father and to him by Apollo were true prophecies, and that they were prophecies fulfilled long ago. Oedipus also understands that every step taken to evade the prophecies – from exposing the infant child to the elements, to his decision never to return to Corinth – was part of the pattern of the fulfillment of the prophecies.

His downfall is tragic. In one moment, Oedipus seems all-powerful and in charge of his destiny. In the next moment, the full weight of his suffering and agonizing self-knowledge renders him completely vulnerable and powerless.

Oedipus rushes into the building after Jocasta. She has hanged herself over their marriage bed. When Oedipus sees his dead wife and mother, he rips the brooches from the shoulder of her gown and stabs out his own eyes with them.

The final resolution, then, is the humbling of the once proud Oedipus. Driven to madness, the willful king accepts his fate by becoming one with it: "*I am agony,*" he says. Shortly thereafter, blind Oedipus wanders out of Thebes into exile.

MYTH OF THE HOUSE OF OEDIPUS

LIMITATIONS OF SELF-KNOWLEDGE

The central theme of *Oedipus the King* is the necessity to understand the limitations of human self-knowledge. Oedipus thinks he knows who he is, but he gets it wrong. He demonstrates how extremely difficult it is to achieve true self-knowledge.

To underscore the theme's importance, Sophocles created a complex and powerful metaphor around the notions of sight and blindness.

Throughout the play, Sophocles sets up a symbolic equivalence between sight and ignorance, blindness and knowledge – exactly the opposite of what you might expect. You would think that sight equals knowledge and that blindness equals ignorance. Not in this play.

The sighted do not know the truth; the blind do know the truth. The only person who knows the truth from the beginning of the play is the blind prophet Tiresias. When Oedipus has sight, he doesn't know who or what he is. When he learns who and what he is, he blinds himself.

The Oedipus story becomes a paradigm for the limitations of human knowledge. To explore that, Sophocles takes the most extreme case possible – a man renowned for wisdom, intelligence and courage. This man is tragically mistaken about the one most basic question that any human being can ever ask – *Who am I?*

Oedipus is the paradigm of any human being who recalls a past tragedy and thinks, "*I should have known earlier. I should have understood, before it was too late. I should have known.*"

FREUD'S INTERPRETATION OF THE OEDIPUS MYTH

The story of Oedipus is arguably the single most famous Greek myth of all. That's due largely to the influence of Sigmund Freud and his use of the Oedipus myth in his psychological theory.

Furthermore, Sophocles' *Oedipus the King* is probably the most often performed Greek tragedy. Countless letters of the alphabet have been forced together in the service of interpreting it. We'll look briefly at only two: the interpretation of Sigmund Freud and the interpretation favored by most modern-day scholars.

Freud read *Oedipus the King* as evidence for his theory of infant sexuality, psychological development, and what he termed the *Oedipus Complex*. He assumed that the play represents subconscious desires. In his view, the play appeals to modern audiences, as it did to ancient ones, as a kind of wish-fulfillment fantasy.

Freud thought that all human beings, as infants, desire sexual union with their opposite-sex parents and desire to be rid of their same-sex parents. His theory holds that we all repress these desires as we grow older, but in *Oedipus the King*, those repressed desires play out in front of us, as we might see them in dreams.

Scholars have raised objections to Freud's reading of the play. First and most obviously, Oedipus is ignorant of his parentage, and that's crucial to the myth. If Oedipus felt oedipal desires, he would have felt them for his adoptive mother Merope, not Jocasta. The whole point is that he doesn't know Jocasta is his mother. He is not working out his repressed infantile oedipal desires by marrying Jocasta. In fact, he's in Thebes precisely to avoid marrying his mother.

Another objection is that Freud asserts that the unconscious and subconscious operate the same way across all cultures and throughout all time. Assume for a moment that Freud's theory is correct about the psychosexual development of children in late 19th- and early 20th-century Vienna.

Even supposing that to be true, one cannot simply extrapolate and assume that the psychosexual development of children works that same way in all cultures at all times, or indeed worked that way in ancient Greece. It is, at least, a questionable assumption, if not a baseless assertion, since Freud offered little or no evidence to support it. In sum, many scholars believe that a Freudian interpretation of *Oedipus the King* is inadequate.

CONFLICT BETWEEN FATE AND FREE WILL

Many believe there exists a more valid interpretation of *Oedipus the King*. That is to view the play's main topic as the conflict between fate and free will.

Laius, Jocasta, and Oedipus are all fated to do the things they do. Apollo's oracle says so. Laius will be murdered by his son. Jocasta will marry and bear children to her son. Oedipus will kill his father and marry his mother. Those things will absolutely happen.

MYTH OF THE HOUSE OF OEDIPUS

And yet, **the inexorable fulfillment of this fate occurs precisely because the characters exercise their free will to try to avoid it.** Although they are fated to commit the deeds they commit, those deeds happen because of the choices the fated ones make, and the course the fated ones take through their own free will.

Throughout the play, **fate and free will interact to bring about what must occur.** Oedipus is a free agent, and he is responsible for the catastrophe. The plot of the play consists not of the actions that were predicted. Rather, the plot consists of Oedipus' discovery that he has already fulfilled the prediction. And this discovery is entirely due to his actions. Oedipus' impulse to fulfill the Delphic admonition to *Know Yourself* drives him to a disastrous outcome.

OEDIPUS: KING AND TRAGIC HERO

Oedipus did have one freedom: he was free to find out, or not find out, the truth. That's the key to the play's tragic theme and key to the protagonist's heroic stature. **One freedom is allowed him: the freedom to search for the whole truth – the truth about the prophecies, about the gods, about himself.** And of this freedom he makes full use.

Against the advice and appeals of others, he pushes on, searching for the truth. In his search, he shows all those qualities for which we admire him – courage, intelligence, and perseverance -- qualities that make human beings great.

This freedom to search, and the heroic way in which Oedipus uses it, make the play a heroic example of man's dedication to the search for the truth about himself. No freedom could be nobler.

OEDIPUS AT COLONUS

In *Oedipus at Colonus*, Sophocles dramatizes the end of the tragic hero's life as well as his mythic significance for Athens.

During the course of the play, Oedipus undergoes a transformation. In the beginning, he is an abject beggar, banished from his city because of his sins. By the end, he has become a figure of immense power, capable of extending (or withholding) divine blessings.

FROM SAVAGERY TO CIVILIZATION

After years of wandering in exile from Thebes, Oedipus arrives in a grove outside Athens. He is a wreck of a man. Blind and frail, he walks with the help of his daughter, Antigone. Oedipus now accepts his fate with resignation.

AS OEDIPUS AT COLONUS OPENS...

Oedipus and Antigone learn from a citizen that they stand on holy ground – a grove sacred to the Eumenides. Recall that those are the sometimes terrible (Furies), sometimes kindly spirits (Eumenides) who rule over unavenged crimes, especially within families.

Oedipus springs to life when he hears this. Oedipus has reason to believe that the Eumenides have taken pity on him. According to the oracle, this grove will be his resting place. Finally he's here, and he refuses to move.

Oedipus sends the citizen to fetch Theseus, the king of Athens. Oedipus tells Antigone that, earlier in his life, when Apollo prophesied his doom, the god promised Oedipus that he would come to rest on this ground.

After an interlude in which Oedipus tells the chorus who he is, Oedipus' second daughter, Ismene, enters. She brings news from Apollo's Oracle at Delphi. She tells Oedipus that, back in Thebes, Oedipus' younger son, Eteocles, has overthrown his older son, Polynices. Polynices is now amassing troops. He means to attack his brother and Creon, who rules along with Eteocles.

The conflict in Thebes — Polynices' battle to take the city by force from Creon and Eteocles — arises from the power vacuum created by Oedipus' downfall. Long ago, Creon banished Oedipus. Eteocles and Polynices did nothing to stop Creon or help Oedipus. Now, because of the prophecy, everyone wants him back. Paradoxically, the Theban curse will be a blessing of victory to Athens, whose king will offer Oedipus burial.

The oracle has predicted that the burial place of Oedipus will bring good fortune to the city in which it is located. Both sons, as well as Creon, know of this prophecy. Both Polynices and Creon are currently in route to take Oedipus into custody and thus claim the right to bury him in their kingdoms. Oedipus swears he will never support either of his sons, for they did nothing to prevent his exile years ago.

This episode sets up the problem of the play — a family's fight over their father's dead body, even while he still lives. King Theseus arrives and expresses pity for the fate that has befallen Oedipus. He asks how he can help. Oedipus asks Theseus to harbor him in Athens until his death, but warns that Theseus will incur the wrath of Thebes by doing Oedipus this favor.

Theseus asks why Thebes and Athens should ever come to war. Oedipus answers with all the authority of his own horrendous experience. He describes the instability of life and earthly circumstances:

Oh Theseus,
Dear friend, only the gods can never age,
the gods can never die. All else in the world
almighty Time obliterates, crushes all
to nothing. The earth's strength wastes away,
the strength of a man's body wastes and dies –
faith dies, and bad faith comes to life,
and the same wind of friendship cannot blow forever,
holding steady and strong between two friends,
much less between two cities.
For some of us soon, for others later,
Joy turned to hate and back again to love.
    — *Oedipus at Colonus*, Lines 685-696. Robert Fagles translation.

Despite Oedipus' warning, Theseus grants Oedipus Athenian citizenship and leaves him under the protection of the elders.

THREATS OF WAR: THREE PRINCIPALS

The next scene moves from polite conversation to threats of war. It dramatizes the three principals in the play: Oedipus, the suffering victim of his fate; Theseus, the fair-minded decisive leader of Athens; and Creon, the bully from Thebes.

Creon appears in order to abduct Oedipus. When Theseus accuses Creon of unlawful action, Creon justifies himself by citing the many sins Oedipus committed. Oedipus, in turn, vigorously defends himself. He insists that he was condemned by the gods to his fate, that he committed his crimes unknowingly, and that he discovered their significance too late. He is determined with his outraged defense to give the gift of his grave, and with it the power of his blessing, to the city he himself chooses – Athens.

Neither Creon nor anyone else contests this defense. Oedipus is cleared of any moral guilt -- in his own eyes and in the eyes of Athens. He is still, however, a polluted being, stained with his father's blood. In ancient Greek belief, the act of killing, even with no blame attached to it, cuts a man off from communion with his fellow men. Only ritual purification can confer a sort of absolution. But for Oedipus, the facts of patricide and incest are beyond purification. He is indeed a polluted being and will go to the grave still an untouchable (to anyone except his daughters, who are the fruits of his incest).

In response, the elders side with Oedipus, whom they now see as innocent of sin, although cursed by ill fortune. The preparation for Oedipus' elevation to divine status at the end of the play now begins.

POLYNICES SEEKS FATHER'S FAVOR

Oedipus must face one more trial, one more test of his heroic resolution. He must confront his son Polynices, who challenges his choice of Athens as his burial place.

Soon after, Polynices arrives. He seeks his father's favor. But Oedipus fiercely upbraids Polynices for neglecting the duties of a son to his father and for allowing him to be sent into exile. Oedipus not only refuses to help Polynices capture Thebes, he prophesies disaster for the expedition.

Here is his curse:

> *Impossible – you'll never tear that city down. No,*
> *you'll fall first, red with your brother's blood*
> *and he stained with yours – equals, twins in blood.*
>
> — *Oedipus at Colonus*, Lines 1554-56. Robert Fagles translation.

He predicts that Eteocles and Polynices will die at one another's hands. Polynices, realizing he will never win his father's support, turns to his sisters. He asks that they provide him with a proper burial should he die in battle. (This line becomes important in the next play, *Antigone*.) Polynices then leaves for Thebes.

OEDIPUS SUMMONED BY THE GODS

A clap of thunder sounds; Oedipus is being summoned by the gods. He says his time of death has come. Now purged of his anger, Oedipus speaks in calm, commanding tones. He understands that the culmination of his fate is at hand. He has reached his resting place and will gift his tomb to Athens.

Theseus must be with him in his last moments, to receive the gift. He is told that he must never reveal Oedipus' burial spot, but to pass that secret on to his son at his own death. The son must in turn pass it on to his own son. In this way, Theseus and his heirs may always rule over a safe city. Oedipus then strides off with sudden strength, leading his daughters and Theseus to his grave.

Before Oedipus goes to his eternal home, however, the gods speak to him. Apart from the prophecies of Apollo, these are the only words the gods speak in either play. *"You, you there, Oedipus — what are we waiting for? / You hold us back too long! We must move on, move on!"* — *Oedipus at Colonus*, Lines 1844-45. Robert Fagles translation.

Although Oedipus does not become a god, that use of the word *we* defines him as no longer human. He belongs to those unseen powers. They preside in mysterious ways over the destinies of men.

DRAMA OF TRANSFORMATION

A messenger enters to narrate the mysterious death of Oedipus: his death seemed a disappearance of sorts, *"the lightless depths of Earth bursting open in kindness to receive him."* — *Oedipus at Colonus*, Lines 1886-87. Robert Fagles translation.

This final scene emphasizes that the play is a drama of transformation, the completion of a rite of passage. Oedipus is transformed from a blind beggar — cast out and reviled as society's ultimate sinner — to a heroic figure, sanctified and at one with the gods. The final mystical scene demonstrates the heroic stature and dignity that one can achieve, despite — or perhaps because of — human suffering in an incomprehensible world.

This is certainly no happy ending, nor was it meant to be. Oedipus has become a protective hero of the Athenian land, with power over his enemies. That is perhaps recognition on the part of the gods that they had used him hard, and that it had cost him incomprehensible suffering. Why did they do that? Perhaps it was to demonstrate, in an extreme example, that human knowledge at its greatest is ignorance compared with theirs. The best way forward for man is cautious humility.

ANTIGONE

The action of *Antigone* begins just after the bloody siege of Thebes by Polynices and his allies. The city stands, unconquered. However, Polynices and his brother Eteocles, the two sons of Oedipus' incestuous marriage, are both dead. They killed each other in single combat, just as the curse of Oedipus had foretold.

Creon, the uncle of Eteocles and Polynices, is now king of Thebes, since all of Oedipus' male heirs are dead. Creon has decreed that Eteocles, the bold defender of Thebes, will be buried with full honor and ceremony.

TERRIBLE PUNISHMENT FOR POLYNICES

However, Creon also decreed that the body of Polynices must be left to rot, to lie unburied and untouched, for dogs and wild birds to tear apart. Creon has further decreed that anyone who disobeys this edict, and buries Polynices, will suffer the penalty of death.

This is a terrible punishment for Polynices. The Greeks felt strongly that the soul of a body left unburied could not make its way into Tartarus, the home of dead souls. (You may recall that this is the same punishment Achilles initially brought down on Hector near the end of the *Iliad*. Achilles dragged Hector's corpse before the gates of Troy for nine days.)

In Greek mythology, the underworld was undoubtedly an unpleasant place to be. It was a grim and gray existence. However, even worse was to be caught in an everlasting in-between state, neither dead nor alive, condemned to an eternity of irresolution.

MYTH OF THE HOUSE OF OEDIPUS
ANTIGONE BURIES POLYNICES

Outside the city gates, Antigone reveals to her sister Ismene a plan to bury Polynices in secret, despite Creon's order. Ismene timidly refuses to defy the king. Antigone angrily goes off alone to bury her brother. Creon discovers that someone has attempted a ritual burial for Polynices. He demands that the guilty one be found and brought before him. When he discovers that Antigone, his niece, is the one defying his order, Creon is furious.

Antigone argues passionately that Creon disobeys the laws of the gods themselves with his decree. Creon in turn is enraged by Antigone's refusal to submit to his authority. He declares that she and her sister will be put to death.

Haemon, Creon's son, was to marry Antigone. He advises his father to reconsider his decision. Father and son argue. Haemon accuses Creon of being arrogant. Creon accuses Haemon of unmanly weakness because he sides with a woman. Haemon leaves in anger, swearing never to return.

Without admitting that Haemon may be right, Creon amends his pronouncement on the sisters: Ismene shall be allowed to live. But Antigone will be sealed in a tomb to die of starvation, rather than the customary punishment of being stoned to death by Theban citizenry.

The blind prophet Tiresias warns Creon that the gods disapprove of his leaving Polynices unburied. They will punish the king's impiety; his own son will die. Creon angrily rejects Tiresias, but then reconsiders a second time. He decides to bury Polynices and free Antigone.

But Creon's change of heart comes too late. Antigone has hanged herself, and Haemon, in desperate agony, has killed himself as well. On hearing the news of her son's death, Eurydice, the queen, also curses Creon and kills herself.

Alone, in despair, Creon accepts responsibility for all the tragedy. He prays for a quick death. The play ends with a somber warning from the chorus that pride will be punished by the blows of fate.

FROM SAVAGERY TO CIVILIZATION

INTERPRETING ANTIGONE

The conflict between Creon and Antigone is not a matter of one being absolutely right and the other absolutely wrong. Much can be said for and against each side.

Their conflict epitomizes the conflict between the claims of the family and the claims of the community. Antigone believes that her loyalty to her immediate family must override all other claims. In this, she follows the expected allegiances of a woman. She acts as a woman should act, but she pushes it to a dangerous extreme.

Creon, on the other hand, believes that the claims of the city are all-important to him. His loyalty and duty to the community must override all other claims. In this he follows the expected allegiances of a man, but pushes them to a dangerous extreme.

The conflict is laid out very clearly, and both sides are pushed to an extreme. Antigone undervalues her duty to her city and its ruler. Creon undervalues his duty to his family. Yet the categories of community and family are interwoven here. Creon is Antigone's uncle, as well as her king. Antigone is Creon's niece and future daughter-in-law, as well as his subject. Each of them finds in the other both family and community.

CREON IS LEGITIMATE RULER

It's a mistake to characterize Creon as an out-and-out villain, as some have. As king, his primary duty is to protect his city. Polynices had attacked his own city and caused a civil war – the worst kind of war because all the victims are from the same community. Creon's edict is meant to display the abhorrent nature of such an act and to deter others.

Creon is the legitimate ruler of Thebes. As king, he demands that everyone obey his edict, because it is the law. He cannot allow citizens to pick and choose which laws they want to obey. His edict is law, and the citizens, therefore, must obey it no matter what they think of it. No one questions his right to rule. However, Creon's position, if taken to the extreme, would amount to totalitarianism, while also defying the gods' commands.

MYTH OF THE HOUSE OF OEDIPUS
ANTIGONE NOT UNAMBIGUOUSLY ADMIRABLE

It is also a mistake to see Antigone as someone to be unambiguously admired. She would have made the original audience very uncomfortable. She is a young unmarried girl (about 14 years old) who directly and intentionally defies the head of her household. As a citizen, she defies the king. As a woman, she defies male authority. And her position, carried to the extreme, would be anarchy.

Antigone's reason for this three-fold act of defiance is that she thinks Creon had no right to issue the edict in the first place. She thinks his edict was unjust. And she says quite clearly that she holds herself bound by the gods' laws, not by Creon's laws. When Creon asks her if she knew of the edict telling her that she must not bury her brother, she says,

Well aware. How could I avoid it? It was public.

He then asks,

And still you had the gall to break this law?

Antigone responds:

> *Of course I did. It wasn't Zeus, not in the least,*
> *who made this proclamation — not to me.*
> *Nor did that Justice, dwelling with the gods*
> *beneath the earth, ordain such laws for men.*
> *Nor did I think your edict had such force*
> *that you, a mere mortal, could override the gods,*
> *the great unwritten, unshakable traditions.*
> *They are alive, not just today or yesterday:*
> *they live forever, from the first of time,*
> *and no one knows when they first saw the light.*
>
> — *Antigone*, Lines 497-508. Robert Fagles translation.

Antigone finds herself bound by higher laws, the laws of the gods, rather than by Creon's laws.

Creon thinks that the law must be obeyed, whether an individual agrees with it or not. Antigone thinks that her individual understanding of the gods' laws supersedes human laws.

This may be the first drama on the topic of civil disobedience. Antigone breaks the law and has every intention of paying the penalty for breaking the law, perhaps foreshadowing Socrates' famous self-sacrifice some 60 years later.

GODS SIDE WITH ANTIGONE

Although there is right and wrong on both sides of this issue, Sophocles makes it quite clear which way the balance falls.

When the seer Tiresias tells Creon that the gods are angry and refusing to accept sacrifices, Creon realizes that he has violated a divine law. He should not have issued an edict forbidding the burial of Polynices, and he should not have condemned Antigone to a cave. Creon's crime was confusing the world of the living with the world of the dead. He committed two outrages, each of which is hateful in the eyes of the gods.

First, he left a dead man unburied, that is, he left Polynices, who belongs to the world of the dead, present in the world of the living. Second and equally awful, Creon walled up the living Antigone in a cave that is, in effect, a tomb. He put a living person in the world of the dead.

CREON FORGOT LIMITATIONS OF HUMAN POWER

Creon comes to realize his crucial mistake. He forgot the limitations of human power. As king, Creon has the right to pass laws about anything that occurs under the jurisdiction of a human king.

But he has forgotten the difference between human and divine authority. He thought that his authority extended to laws that, as Antigone told him, belong to the gods and not to humans. The necessity of burying the dead is a commandment belonging to the realm of the gods and is based on their authority.

That was Creon's crucial mistake. He thought he had absolute power over issues that no human has power over. Unfortunately, he understood this too late and was unable to rectify his mistake. Antigone, Haemon, and Eurydice all died because of Creon's poor judgment.

ANTIGONE — A DISTURBING CHARACTER

And so, in estimating the relative power of human and divine law, Antigone was right. Nevertheless, Antigone is still a very disturbing character. The Chorus is quite clearly uncomfortable with her.

They remark on her stubbornness and her unyielding nature, which, they say, led her to being imprisoned in a cave.

Antigone is exactly what the critic Bernard Knox referred to when he reminded us that Sophoclean heroes are called *deinos*, that term we discussed briefly in *Oedipus the King*. The word means wonderful, terrible, and strange. And for Antigone as *deinos*, it means that she is simultaneously wondrous and awe-inspiring and terrible and frightening.

Creon is, in many ways, more understandable, likable, and human than Antigone. At first the scales seemed to be weighted in his favor. As a male, head of the household and legitimate ruler, he would likely expect that right would be more on his side than on Antigone's. This shows just how difficult it can be to know the bounds of one's duty to community, family, and the gods.

LESSONS OF ANTIGONE

The play demonstrates that the gods' laws are paramount, and that human power is limited. The Chorus says that a man and his city do well, when he manages to weave together *"the laws of the land, and justice of the gods."*

That points directly to the conflict of the play, namely, the difficulty of weaving together the laws of man and the justice of the gods. And it is a reminder that human intellect is not sufficient to the task in and of itself. The gods' laws must be taken into account, and Creon's suffering at the end of the play is the proof of that.

OEDIPUS' RITE OF PASSAGE

That concludes our reading of Sophocles' Oedipus plays. In the myth of the House of Oedipus, and in Sophocles' treatment of it, we have seen, to a rare degree, human innocence burdened with unmerited human suffering.

These plays are indeed puzzling. Why should Oedipus, who is innocent and unaware, be forced to unknowingly fulfill a horrid prophecy of patricide and incest? And why must Antigone die for doing the right thing — for doing exactly what the gods want her to do? These are perplexing questions. In each case, the misery and tragedy seem unjustified, or completely out of proportion, to their cause.

FROM SAVAGERY TO CIVILIZATION

HEAVEN'S WAYS NOT MAN'S WAYS

Sophocles did face up to this problem. But in the end he could only say that the ways of heaven are not man's ways, and that undeserved suffering is inexplicable by human standards. At the same time, Sophocles still maintained his faith in the gods, even if he couldn't understand them.

Above all, though, Sophocles maintained his faith in man — he who bears up under terrible agony and still retains his humanity. This comes across most clearly in Oedipus' death and transfiguration. Oedipus is granted a special dispensation from the gods after having braved a merciless fate. Like all fates once imposed, remember, his fate was unchangeable; even the gods could not contravene it.

In some ways, Oedipus may seem a different kind of hero, but we have witnessed his like before. Although Oedipus is bold, resourceful, and intelligent, his outstanding trait is his ability to suffer. After blundering into a deadly trap set by the gods, he accepts the responsibility for the sins he committed in innocence. He blinds himself and resigns his throne. He then undergoes years of torment, and, at last, at the completion of this rite of passage, he emerges purified and immortal.

ANCIENT GREEK RITES OF PASSAGE

Initiation, suffering, death, atonement, and redemption or immortality. These were the elements of the rites of passage Greek heroes endured. We add Oedipus' rite of passage to the myths of Heracles, Achilles, Odysseus, the House of Atreus, and others.

The most important element in a rite of passage among these heroes was the profound, out-of-proportion, gut-wrenching suffering, imposed in a world dominated by unchangeable fate.

Only the ancient Greeks could understand the suffering that fate forced their heroes to endure, in order to gain redemption, immortality, or a more civilized society. Indeed, only the unsparingly honest Greeks could have created, or even understood, the fate-imposed pain and anguish laid bare in the story of the House of Oedipus.

MYTH OF THE HOUSE OF OEDIPUS

Here are Sophocles' final words on the subjects of fate and suffering:
The mighty words of the proud are paid in full
with mighty blows of fate, and at long last
those blows will teach us wisdom.
— *Antigone,* Lines 1468-1470. Robert Fagles translation.

And so we come to the end of our examination of the Greek myths. These, of course, are just a few of many they created to tell their stories. In the end, ancient Greece's many myths coalesce into one story of their society's singular cultural rite of passage — from savagery to civilization.

The ROMANS BORROWED GREEK MYTHOLOGY, and much else, and adapted it to their own uses. Their chief god was Mars, god of war. Mars served Rome well during its centuries of empire building. Supreme ruler Jupiter played a secondary role among the Romans.

CHAPTER XI
ROMAN FOUNDATION MYTHS

WE WILL NOW SWITCH CIVILIZATIONS — FROM GREEK TO ROMAN. As we noted early on, classical mythology is so-called because the Greeks created the myths, and the Romans borrowed them. The same myths appear in both Greek and Roman literature and art.

Rome not only borrowed the Greeks' mythology. It also adapted to its own uses several other Greek categories: culture, philosophy, rhetoric, history, epic, tragedy, their forms of art, their method of creating statuary, and more. In all of these areas, Rome borrowed from Greece and modified Greek originals to its own purposes.

This was a very unusual situation, so why did it happen? Mostly because of the chronology of the two cultures and their close geography (only the Adriatic Sea separates them). Greece was the first culture; Rome the second.

CHRONOLOGY OF TWO CULTURES

The zenith of Greek culture (500 — 400 BC) preceded the peak of Roman culture (100 BC – 100 AD) by more than 500 years. Over those centuries, Rome gradually gained in importance in the Mediterranean world; Alexander the Great came, conquered and died; and Greece waned in both power and influence under both.

In the fourth century BC, after the high point of the fifth century, King Philip of Macedonia, and later his son, Alexander the Great, dominated Athens and Greece. Alexander the Great's death in 323 BC marked the end of the Classical Age in Greece. That was followed by the Hellenistic Age – the period from 323 BC to 31 BC – during which Greece produced a great deal of literature and art.

In 146 BC, Rome conquered Greece in the Battle of Corinth. Greece became a Roman province. The Battle of Actium in 31 BC ended the Roman Republic and the Hellenistic Age, and marked the beginning of the Roman Empire.

FROM SAVAGERY TO CIVILIZATION

Throughout this period of several centuries, as Greece waned in political power and Rome's influence expanded, Roman and Greek cultures regularly interacted with one another. Romans were continually exposed to Greek cultural forms and artifacts – their literature, drama, art, statuary, and so on.

ROMAN GODS WERE PRACTICAL

As a rule, the Romans were not myth-makers, and the myths they held to were usually imported. The Roman gods were utilitarian, like the practical Romans themselves. Their gods were expected to serve and protect men. When they failed to be useful, their worship was curtailed.

The Romans didn't lack religious sentiment, but they had a pantheistic sense of the divinities present in nature. Their deepest religious feelings centered on the family and the state.

The Romans adopted the Greek gods, and then simplified them to conform to the Roman religion. They gave most of the Greek deities Roman names, and they manipulated Greek myths to reflect Roman views and values. Mars (Ares to the Greeks), god of war, was the chief god of the Roman imperial age. He was more honored than Jupiter (Zeus), since he aided and symbolized the Roman conquests. The writers who handled mythological subjects typically dealt with patriotic legends that glorified the Roman past or with love tales. Thus they paid tribute to the state or to love, the basis of the family, in terms derived from Greek mythology. Sometimes in their borrowings they achieved true originality, as Virgil did in the *Aeneid* and Ovid in the *Metamorphoses*.

In one of the strangest cultural borrowings, Rome took over most of Greece's religion, and especially its mythology. As far as historians can tell, no other human culture has failed to develop its own gods. Actually, the Romans didn't fail either, but their native Roman gods tended to be minor, local deities.

The Romans assimilated the Greeks' major deities – the Olympians, the A-list gods with the most impressive lineages – with their native gods. These adaptations are evident in Virgil's treatment of the Trojan War myth in the *Aeneid*. The Romans manipulated the Greek myth of the Trojan War to fit their own cultural needs.

ROMAN FOUNDATION MYTHS

AENEAS — ANCESTOR OF THE ROMAN PEOPLE

The Roman tradition about Rome's beginnings, which grew out of the *Aeneid*, was that Aeneas, whose name means *praiseworthy*, was the ancestor of the Roman people. This tradition had its beginnings

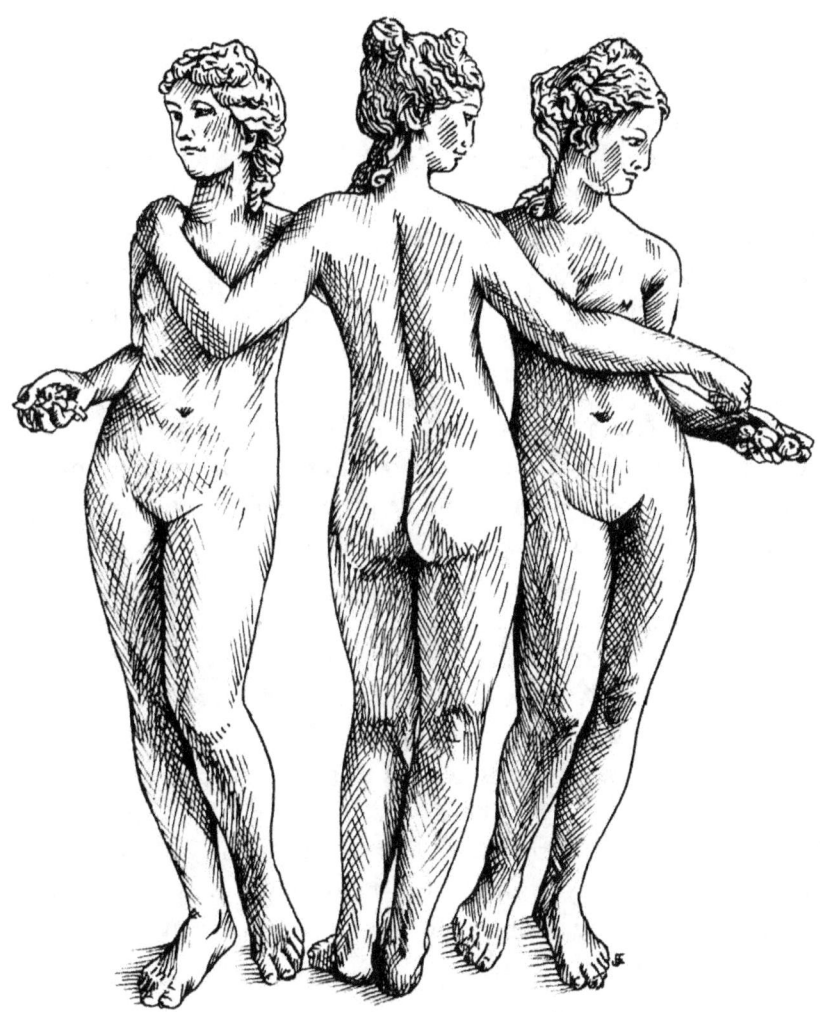

THE THREE GRACES, a Greek masterpiece from the second century AD. The graces dance naked in a circle, each resting a hand on the shoulder of another. The Roman nobility and the government demanded copies of Greek statues such as this to decorate theatres, public baths and monuments.

in Book XX of the *Iliad*. There, the god Poseidon says that Aeneas cannot be killed in battle at that particular moment. He is fated to survive the war, go west, and found another city somewhere else. This became the most prominent example of Roman myth altering. Romans decided that the "other city somewhere else" was in fact Rome.

This became critically important in the stories Romans told themselves about where they came from.

The Romans understood that their culture was much younger than Greece's. Greek myths stretched all the way back to the very beginning of time. The Greeks were a very ancient culture, while the Roman's own native tradition said that their city had been founded in only 753 BC. The Greeks boasted a vast pedigree connecting the families of everyday modern Greece with the heroes and gods of antiquity.

DID ROMANS DESCEND FROM TROJANS?

It was a problem that Roman culture was so much younger than Greek culture. The Romans remedied the problem by identifying themselves with the Trojans in the Trojan War.

By claiming to be the descendants of Trojans, the Romans applied to themselves a pedigree stretching back every bit as far as the Greek pedigree. Suddenly the Romans could tell themselves, "*We were there all along, too. We are as ancient as the Greeks. We were on the other side in the Trojan War, fighting against the Greeks.*"

And so that was the banner the Romans carried forward. In historical fact, however, there is no historical fact. There is absolutely no evidence that survivors of the Trojan War ever made their way west to Italy. And yet, for the Romans the story of the *Aeneid* became a very strong article of faith – an essential part of their self-constructed identity.

CHAPTER XII
ROMULUS AND REMUS

SIDE BY SIDE WITH THE GREEK STORY OF THE TROJAN WAR WERE THE ROMAN LEGENDS ABOUT THE FOUNDING OF THE CITY OF ROME BY ROMULUS. Greek tradition never overcame this strong native Roman tradition, and the legend never went away.

In Virgil's rendering, Aeneas made his way to Italy and became the ancestor of the Roman race. But he didn't actually found the city of Rome. According to the ever malleable Trojan War myth, Romulus was a descendant of Aeneas; Aeneas was his great-great-grandfather. That means that Romans descended from Trojans. Aeneas founded their race. Romulus founded their city.

This version of Roman history/myth provided another benefit. Recall that Aeneas was the child of Aphrodite, borne after her affair with the human Anchises – that's Aphrodite, the Greek goddess of love and a primary Olympian deity. Her Roman name was Venus. So according to the Romans, they too were descended from one of the primary Olympian deities through Aeneas. The Romans were very serious about this. Julius Caesar and his entire family traced their descent back directly to Aeneas, the founder of the Roman race, and Venus, the Roman goddess of love.

LEGENDS OF ROMULUS AND REMUS

But how does Romulus fit in? Romulus was in many ways a typical hero of the type we've seen before. His story contains a number of folktale-like elements. His birth was difficult, for example, and he wasn't recognized as Romulus until after he had grown up and was away from his original home.

As the story goes, Mars, the Roman god of war, ravished the Roman princess, Rhea Silvia, a descendant of Aeneas. This coupling produced twin sons, Romulus and Remus. At birth, their wicked uncle set the pair adrift in a basket on the Tiber River. They washed ashore, and a she-wolf rescued and suckled them as though they were her own cubs. A shepherd then adopted the twins and raised them as his own sons.

When Romulus and Remus reached adulthood, their true lineage was discovered through a series of complicated coincidences. The two reinstated their grandfather on the throne of Alba Longa, the city founded by the descendants of Aeneas.

The two decided to found their own city, which, of course, would be Rome. The brothers quarreled over which of them would name the city and, therefore, rule over it. During the quarrel, Romulus killed Remus and gave his own name to the city. Thus, Rome originated in a fratricide.

(*I personally think that this was the best outcome. What if Remus had won? The city would be called Reem. "All roads lead to Reem?" I don't think so. It doesn't resonate.*)

After founding his city, Romulus gathered around him a group of young men – less-than-upright citizens and refugees from nearby towns. They would now be his citizenry. However, an immediate problem arose. You can't have a city without children and new generations, and you can't have new generations without women. The Roman men needed wives.

A SHE-WOLF RESCUED ROMULUS AND REMUS from the Tiber River and suckled them as though they were her own cubs. A shepherd later found them and raised them as his own children.

To solve this issue, the Romans invited the neighboring tribe, the Sabines, to a religious festival. At a prearranged signal, the young Roman men abducted all the Sabine women and made them their wives.

ROMULUS, FOUNDER OF ROME

So Romulus began his rule over Rome by murdering his brother. He consolidated his rule by violating a religious festival through a mass abduction. It is further proof, if we needed it, that in classical myth, heroes, even heroes who found cities, are not necessarily good men. Romulus was not a good man.

The ambiguous nature of Romulus – the founder of Rome, and yet a violent and treacherous man – may be reflected in the conflicting stories of his death. The Roman historian Livy offers two versions.

The first version is that on a certain day, Romulus was talking to the senators, a government body he had founded. Suddenly, the gods lifted Romulus up bodily in a cloud and carried him up to Mount Olympus and made him a god. That's version one.

In version two, Livy says, the senators, at a prearranged signal, tore Romulus to shreds and hid his body.

(Both of these stories can't possibly be true. One must surely be fake news. You choose.)

So Romulus founded the city of Rome, but it was Aeneas who descended from the Trojans, Aeneas who became the ancestor of the Roman race, and Aeneas who laid the groundwork for Roman civilization. Aeneas is by far the transcendent hero in this legend. That's our segue into discussing Virgil's *Aeneid*....

AENEAS, son of Venus, goddess of love, carries his old and lame father, Anchises, as they flee the flames of falling Troy. According to Virgil, Trojan Aeneas became the ancestor of the Roman race and laid the groundwork for Roman civilization.

CHAPTER XIII
THE AENEID BY VIRGIL

THE AENEID IS THE GREAT NATIONAL EPIC OF ANCIENT ROME, AND ONE OF THE MOST IMPORTANT WORKS OF LITERATURE IN THE WESTERN TRADITION. Within Roman culture, it provided a foundation myth. It formed a link between the Greek mythic tradition and Roman history. Along with only a few others, the *Aeneid* served as one of the basic works of education throughout the Roman Empire until the fall of Rome in 476 AD and beyond.

Because of Rome's massive influence on later European civilization, the *Aeneid* served as the model for a great deal of later literature. During late antiquity and the Middle Ages, Greek was not studied in Western Europe. Thus, the *Aeneid* became the primary source of information about the Trojan War myth.

Virgil had a major influence on subsequent epic writers. In Dante's *Divine Comedy*, for example, Virgil is a guide through hell. He also appears in works by Geoffrey Chaucer, Christopher Marlowe, John Milton, John Dryden and C.S. Lewis.

The divisions in Virgil's underworld, where Aeneas visits on one of his side journeys, seem to prefigure subsequent aspects of Christianity. In late antiquity, the *Aeneid* was one of the most commonly read and cited books for religious education.

St. Augustine, for example, mentions in his *Confessions* that he wept over the death of Queen Dido when he read the *Aeneid* as a child in about 360 AD. Virgil was often called a soul naturally Christian. In particular, he seemed to prophesy the birth of Christ in one of his books.

THE AENEID — OPENING LINES

The *Aeneid* was completed in about 19 BC. It can be divided into two halves based on their different subject matter. Books I-VI tell of Aeneas' journey from Troy to Latium in Italy. Books VII-XII record the war in Latium. These two halves reflect Virgil's ambition to rival

Homer by treating both the *Odyssey's* wandering theme and the *Iliad's* warfare theme. Books I-VI are sometimes referred to as the Roman *Odyssey*. Books VII-XII are the Roman *Iliad*. Here are the opening lines of the *Aeneid*:

> *Wars and a man I sing – an exile driven on by Fate,*
> *he was the first to flee the coast of Troy,*
> *destined to reach Lavinian shores and Italian soil,*
> *yet many blows he took on land and sea from the gods above –*
> *thanks to cruel Juno's relentless rage – and many losses*
> *he bore in battle too, before he could found a city,*
> *bring his gods to Latium, source of the Latin race,*
> *the Alban Lords and the high walls of Rome.*
> *Tell me, Muse, how it all began. Why was Juno outraged?*
> *What could wound the Queen of the Gods with all her power?*
> *Why did she force a man, so famous for his devotion,*
> *to brave such rounds of hardship, bear such trials?*
> *Can such rage inflame immortals' hearts?*
>
> — Book I, Lines 1-11. Robert Fagles translation.

Virgil begins with *"Wars and a man I sing..."* He says he will tell the story of Aeneas, who fled from Troy and whose fate it was to eventually reach Latium in Italy. There, he would found the race that would one day build Rome.

But Aeneas' journey is made difficult by the gods, and especially by Juno, queen of the gods and wife of Jupiter (Hera and Zeus to the Greeks). Virgil wonders why Juno hates Aeneas, who is famous for his piety. He asks the Muse, the goddess of the arts, to tell him about the source of her anger.

Virgil's debts to Homer, and his differences from Homer, are obvious in the first line – *Arma virumque cano ("Wars and a man I sing")*. The first words recall both the *Iliad*, which focuses on warfare, and the *Odyssey*, which centers on the adventures of one man. But Virgil says he will sing of both – of war and a man. This is a story about a hero who faces war.

THE AENEID BY VIRGIL
PURPOSE OF THE AENEID

The *Aeneid* was written in the Augustine Age, that is, during the reign of Caesar Augustus in the first century BC. Virgil intended to provide a mythological background and explanation for Rome's subsequent development.

Written in hindsight, the *Aeneid* no longer meets the definition of myth. It's not a traditional story a society tells itself, which was our operating definition of a myth. Rather, the *Aeneid* is a work of literature – a traditional story created by an individual artist.

The *Aeneid's* larger goal is stressed from the beginning. Aeneas is destined to found Roman civilization, and Roman civilization is destined to be founded by Aeneas. In the *Aeneid*, destiny or fate is not treated the same way as it is in Homeric epics. There, fate certainly plays an important role, but it's largely considered an individual matter. Aeneas' fate is constantly and consistently pictured as leading to the founding of Rome. His individual destiny is in service to the greater goal of his society.

It's also immediately clear that Virgil worked in a different literary tradition than Homer. The *Iliad* and *Odyssey* are the culminations of a centuries-long oral tradition. We do not know exactly when, where, why, or how they came to be written down. The *Aeneid's* opening lines, however, make clear that this is the work of one author, not the product of an oral tradition. Virgil announces his subject in the first-person singular (*"I sing"*), whereas Homer invokes the Muse to sing.

The *Aeneid* is also much more than the story of Aeneas' journey from Troy to Italy. It's a story about a band of survivors who leave their destroyed city to seek another home in a faraway country. It is about rebirth through a painful rite of passage, similar to the rites of passage Greek heroes underwent. It is about life springing forth from ruin and death. It traces a pattern just as profound as any we've seen in Greek myth – the human spirit's eternal quest for redemption and self-perpetuation.

FROM SAVAGERY TO CIVILIZATION

AENEID'S THEMES

As in most of classical mythology, fate is a dominant theme of the *Aeneid*. Aeneas' adventures are driven by fate, and the founding of the Roman race is inevitable.

Another theme is *pietas*, which refers to one's duty and proper behavior toward all those to whom duty is owed. Aeneas is noted for his *pietas*. For Romans it meant being mindful of one's duty to the gods, one's family, and one's country. Further, in Aeneas' case, *pietas* describes his loyalty and duty to Rome and to his mission to establish Roman civilization in Italy.

ANGER OF GODDESS JUNO

We meet the goddess Juno early in the epic. Juno is implacably angry at the Trojans. Several reasons exist for her anger, but, first and foremost, Juno is angry because of the judgment of Paris.

You will recall that, during the judgment of Paris, three goddesses – Athena (Minerva to the Romans), Aphrodite (now Venus), and Hera (now Juno) – competed for the title of most beautiful woman. Paris, the Trojan prince, had to choose, and he chose Venus. His choice led to the abduction of Helen, which led to the Trojan War, and so forth. Paris did not choose Juno, and she never forgave him for that slight.

In fact, Juno's hatred extends beyond Paris to the entire Trojan people. Why? Because the founder of Troy, Dardanus, was one of many illegitimate children sired by her randy husband Jupiter. She especially despises the royal family of Troy, because Jupiter abducted the young Trojan prince Ganymede to be his paramour and cupbearer.

Juno does, however, love Carthage, and she knows that Carthage will eventually cross swords with Rome. But until then, she has vowed to prevent Aeneas from succeeding in his mission to found Roman civilization.

HELP FROM VENUS

Another major deity in the *Aeneid* is Venus, goddess of love and Aeneas' mother. She tries to help her son. She complains to Jupiter about Aeneas' many misfortunes. Jupiter has promised that Romans will one day rule land and sea, Venus reminds him, and that other Trojans have already escaped from the war and settled in new lands. Jupiter reassures her that Aeneas will indeed found a great nation, but only after many trials. This is Aeneas' destiny, and even Juno will become reconciled to it.

Jupiter's answer establishes the supreme god as the arbiter of *fate*, and reasserts the inevitability of Rome's power. His words seem to imply that *fate*, and what he has decreed, are more or less the same thing. He prophesies the coming of a descendent of Venus who will bring power and peace to Rome, a *Trojan Caesar* named Julius. That most likely refers to Caesar Augustus.

AENEAS SETS SAIL FOR ITALY

The action of the *Aeneid* begins with the Trojan fleet in the eastern Mediterranean, sailing toward Italy. The fleet, led by Aeneas, is on a voyage to find a second home. It has been foretold that in Italy he will give rise to a noble and courageous race that will become known to all nations.

The Trojan-hating goddess Juno sees an opportunity to take revenge. She bribes Aeolus, king of the winds, to stir up a storm. Aeolus complies and devastates Aeneas' fleet.

Neptune (the Greek Poseidon), god of the sea, takes notice. He becomes angry because Juno has intruded into his domain. He stills the winds and calms the waters. The fleet takes shelter at Carthage on the coast of Africa, near what is today Tunisia.

There, while recovering from the storm, Venus, disguised as a Carthaginian huntress, recounts for Aeneas the history of Queen Dido and Carthage. Dido is a princess who fled her home in Phoenicia (modern day Lebanon). She is an impressive woman – beautiful, independent and intelligent. Her people respect her.

She is building a new city in Carthage, making her own laws, and directing the work. The temple to Juno, still under construction, demonstrates her love of art. It features pictures of the Trojan War, including pictures of Aeneas himself. Carthage will later become a great imperial rival and enemy to Rome.

FROM SAVAGERY TO CIVILIZATION

AENEAS AND QUEEN DIDO

Aeneas ventures into the city to present himself to Queen Dido. At the same time, each for her own reasons, Juno and Venus plot for a love affair to blossom between Aeneas and Dido. Venus sends Cupid (in the form of Ascanius, Aeneas' young son) to present Dido with gifts. That is about all it takes. Before the night is over, Dido has fallen in love – first with the child, perhaps, and then with the child's father.

AENEAS' STORY: THE FALL OF TROY

That evening, at a banquet hosted by Dido, Aeneas sadly recounts how he and his fellow Trojans have come to arrive at Carthage. His tale begins in Troy shortly before the end of the Trojan War.

In the final campaign of the war, Aeneas begins, the Trojans were tricked into accepting a wooden horse within their city walls. The Greeks built the wooden horse, filled its hollow belly with their best warriors, and placed it before the Trojan gates.
They sailed their fleet to a nearby island out of sight of Troy.

The Trojans assumed that the Greeks had gone for good and reacted with joy. They were astonished by the horse but unsure what to do with it. Some thought it should be taken inside the city. Others thought it should be destroyed. Laocoon, a priest of Neptune, advised against accepting the horse. He coined the famous phrase, "*I fear Greeks bearing gifts.*"

The Trojans then took the horse inside the fortified walls. After nightfall the armed Greeks emerged from the belly of the horse and opened the city's gates. The returned Greek army overwhelmed the city and slaughtered the Trojans.

In a dream, Venus advised Aeneas to flee with his family. Aeneas awoke and watched with horror as Troy was destroyed. He witnessed the murder of King Priam by the son of Achilles. At first he tried to fight the enemy, but soon all his Trojan comrades had fallen. He was left alone to fend off the Greeks.

Venus appeared and led him back to his house. Various omens warned him to flee. Ascanius' head caught fire, for example, without his being harmed. They heard claps of thunder and saw a shooting star.

THE AENEID BY VIRGIL

Aeneas escaped with Ascanius and his father, Anchises. After fleeing Troy, he returned for his wife, Creusa, but she had been killed. Her ghost urged him to fulfill his destiny and found a new city in the West.

WANDERINGS OF AENEAS

After Troy fell, Aeneas led a small group of Trojans away. He built a fleet and searched for a site on which to establish a new city. He landed on several islands, including Crete; he also went ashore in Greece and Italy.

At each stop, the gods urged him to move on and not build there. Or the local inhabitants became hostile, and staying seemed too risky. Or the alluring local inhabitant would delay his journey too long if he lingered.

The fleet sailed on. He landed on the Strophades Islands, the land of the Harpies, and departed quickly. At Buthrotum, on the west coast of Greece, he met other survivors of the war, including Helenus, one of Priam's sons, who had the gift of prophecy. Through Helenus, Aeneas learned for the first time with certainty the destiny laid out for him: he was divinely chosen to find Italy. There, his descendants would prosper and in time rule the known world.

Aeneas made his way nearly to Sicily. There, his ships were caught in the whirlpool of Charybdis and driven out to sea. They came ashore at the land of the Cyclops, and then barely escaped. Finally, Aeneas' storm-ravaged fleet collapsed on the shores of Carthage.

AENEAS AND DIDO IN LOVE

Aeneas finishes his story, and Dido realizes that she has fallen in love with him. Juno makes a deal with Venus that requires Aeneas to remain in Carthage. Juno hopes to distract Aeneas from fulfilling his destiny.

The next day, Aeneas and Dido go hunting. The gods send a storm that forces them to shelter in a cave. Aeneas and Dido have sex. With this union, Dido considers herself to be married. Although Aeneas does not share this view, Aeneas and Dido remain together until Aeneas leaves Carthage.

Finally, Jupiter sends Mercury (Greek Hermes, messenger of the gods) to remind Aeneas of his duty. In secret, the hero reluctantly

FROM SAVAGERY TO CIVILIZATION

makes plans to depart. Dido learns of his plans, becomes angry, and pleads with him to stay. Her words are useless. The will of the gods must be obeyed. Aeneas has no choice but to leave.

Dido's heart is broken. She commits suicide by stabbing herself with Aeneas' sword atop a funeral pyre. Before dying, she correctly predicts eternal strife between Rome and Carthage. Looking back from the deck of his ship, Aeneas sees the smoke of Dido's funeral pyre and understands its meaning. Nevertheless, destiny calls. The Trojan fleet sails to Italy.

BOOK V — REST ON SICILY

In Book V, the fleet stops on Sicily to rest. Aeneas organizes a series of games — a boat race, foot race, boxing match, and archery contest. Each contest comments on past events or prefigures future events. The boxing match, for example, is a preview of the final encounter between Aeneas and Turnus at the end of the epic.

Afterwards, Ascanius leads the boys in a military parade and mock battle. Aeneas will teach this tradition to the Latins while building the walls of Alba Longa, his new city.

During these events (in which only men participate), Juno incites the women to burn the fleet and prevent the Trojans from ever reaching Italy. Ascanius and Aeneas intervene, thwarting her plan. Aeneas prays to Jupiter to quench the fires. The god calls down a torrential rainstorm.

In a dream, Aeneas' father, who died earlier in the journey, directs him to travel to the underworld to receive a vision of his and Rome's future. In return for safe passage across the sea, Neptune orders Aeneas to sacrifice one of his men. Aeneas turns to Palinurus, the night steersman on his ship. Palinurus is a very capable steersman and all-around good guy. He is always willing to help out. So they sacrifice him.

BOOK VI — AENEAS TRAVELS TO THE UNDERWORLD

In Book VI, Aeneas, with the guidance of Sibyl, the priestess at the Oracle at Cumae, descends into the underworld to visit his father. He is shown a pageant of the future history and heroes of Rome.

He meets the spirits of those who died in the Trojan War, those who will later become important people in Rome, the kings of Rome who will give Rome her laws, and Augustus who will become the first Roman emperor. Viewing this pageant helps Aeneas understand the importance of his mission and places it in proper historical perspective. He returns from the underworld, and the Trojans continue up the coast to the Latium region of Italy.

BOOKS VII-XII — WAR IN ITALY

The second half of the *Aeneid*, Books VII-XII, is sometimes referred to as the Roman *Iliad* and takes place in Italy.

Virgil describes the second half as the *greater theme* and the *greater labor* in his invocation to the Muse Erato. This story is now on home territory for Virgil and his original readers. The second half of the *Aeneid* references local towns, customs, legends, etc. Book VII balances Book I and serves as a fitting second beginning for the poem.

Book VII marks the start of the second part of the *Aeneid*. The wandering is over; the war begins. Aeneas establishes a settlement in Latium, after gaining permission from local King Latinus. The king is convinced that the Trojans are favored by destiny and so wants to be on the right side of history. So he cooperates.

However, in his efforts to help, Latinus is frustrated by his own subjects. One subject, the Rutulian Prince Turnus, does not trust Aeneas and wants to force the Trojans out of Latium. Latinus' wife, Amata, agrees with Turnus. She wants him to marry their daughter, Lavinia. At the same time, the goddess Juno plots for a war to break out between Aeneas and Turnus.

WAR BREAKS OUT

When war between the Trojans and the Latins becomes inevitable, Aeneas enlists the help of Evander, king of Pallantium (site of the future Rome). The battles begin and soon reach full fury. Many warriors are slain on both sides.

In Books XI and XII, the Trojans gain the upper hand. The narrative begins to build inexorably toward Turnus' death at Aeneas' hands. Jupiter forbids any further interference by Juno, and she reluctantly yields. But she seeks an answer to a question often asked in subsequent centuries: *Whatever happened to the name Trojans among the Romans?*

Here's Juno's request:

> *Never command the Latins, here on native soil,*
> *to exchange their age-old name,*
> *to become Trojans....*
> *Let Latium endure. Let Alban kings hold sway for all time.*
> *Let Roman stock grow strong with Italian strength.*
> *Troy has fallen — and fallen let her stay —*
> *with the very name of Troy!*

And Jupiter grants her wish:

> *Latium's sons will retain their fathers' words and ways.*
> *Their name till now is the name that shall endure.*
> *Mingling in stock alone, the Trojans will subside.*
> *And I will add the rites and the forms of worship,*
> *and make them Latins all, who speak one Latin tongue.*
>
> — Book XII, Lines 954-971. Robert Fagles translation.

FINAL SCENE: AENEAS VS TURNUS

On the battlefield, things go badly for Turnus and the Rutulians. Finally, rather than sue for peace, Turnus challenges Aeneas to single combat. The winner will marry Lavinia, and the war will end.

Before the duel begins, Venus equips her son with new arms and shield, forged by the smith-god Vulcan (Greek Hephaestus). The entire history of Rome is pictured across its surface — from the she-wolf who suckled Romulus and Remus, to the Battle of Actium many years in the future, which will make Augustus master of the world.

The two warriors fight for a long time. Finally, Aeneas' spear punctures Turnus' thigh. Turnus begs on his knees for his life. At first, Aeneas is tempted to be merciful. However, Turnus killed Aeneas' close friend in battle and now shoulders the man's trophy belt. Aeneas, seeing this, kills Turnus in a rage. And so ends the war and the epic.

AENEAS: EPIC HERO, ARCHETYPAL ROMAN

The *Aeneid* is not a personal epic about Aeneas. Instead it's a national epic – a glorification of Rome and a saga about the destiny of the Roman people.

The poem is about Aeneas' role in founding the Roman state. It's also about Aeneas' embodiment of Roman personal qualities, especially the Roman sense of duty and responsibility.

Virgil viewed Rome as majestic, sacred, and ordained by destiny to rule the world. In his mind, superhuman forces control all human affairs. They ordained that Rome would attain the greatness about which he wrote.

Thus, the *Aeneid* exalts Rome and shows the imprint of the divine and fate in its existence. It also glorifies the finest features of the city by their personification in Aeneas.

Aeneas is Rome's epic hero, finally, as well as her archetypal citizen.

PYRAMUS AND THISBE, the prototype myth of the Romeo and Juliet story made famous by Shakespeare. The story is not found anywhere before Ovid. Is it a genuine ancient Greek myth or simply a creation of Ovid?

CHAPTER XIV
METAMORPHOSES BY OVID

THE METAMORPHOSES IS OVID'S GREAT MYTHOLOGICAL WORK. In it, he focuses on the classical myths inherited by the Romans from the Greeks. The stories are our primary source, and many times our only source, for some of the most famous classical myths.

The *Metamorphoses* (meaning *transformations*) is a narrative poem in 15 books and includes more than 250 myths. It was completed in AD 8. It is an epic or mock epic poem describing the creation and history of the world. It incorporates many of the best known stories from Greek mythology, although it centers more on human characters than on heroes or gods. The link tying all the stories together is the transformation (or metamorphosis) that occurs in each one.

As examples, *Metamorphoses* provides us with the fullest accounts we have of the stories of Apollo and Daphne, Phaethon, and Narcissus.

APOLLO AND DAPHNE

Daphne was a nymph and the daughter of a river god. Nymphs were intermediate beings between gods and humans. Apollo's younger brother, Cupid, struck Apollo with an arrow, cursing him with an overwhelming desire for Daphne. He wanted to marry Daphne, or at least mate with her, but Daphne had vowed to remain a virgin forever.

Apollo tried to catch her, but she ran away. Daphne prayed for help from her father, and he transformed her into a laurel tree. Apollo then made the laurel his sacred tree. Thereafter, Apollo wore a wreath of laurel leaves on his head, and that became one of his common attributes.

This brief description of the myth lacks contextual details and raises questions. Other relevant details about Apollo and Daphne that might fill the gaps or answer the questions either don't exist or have been ignored. We find this story only in Ovid, who told us only what he wanted us to hear.

FROM SAVAGERY TO CIVILIZATION
FALL OF PHAETHON

Another story we know of mainly from Ovid is the story of Phaethon. He was the son of Apollo, in Apollo's role as sun god, and of a mortal mother.

Phaethon wondered whether the sun god really was his father. So he journeyed to the palace of the sun god in the remote East and asked him, "*If you truly are my father, promise on the River Styx that you will grant me my one request.*"

Apollo made the promise. Phaethon's one request was to drive the chariot of the sun across the sky for one whole day. Apollo knew that such an attempt would be fatal. He tried to reason with the boy. He told Phaethon that no other god, not even Jupiter himself, could drive this chariot.

But Phaethon insisted. Since Apollo had promised by the River Styx, he could not renege on his promise. He allowed the boy to drive the chariot.

But when Phaethon was placed in charge of the chariot, he couldn't control the horses. The earth was in danger of being burnt up because of Phaethon's mishandling. To prevent disaster, Zeus struck down the chariot with a thunderbolt, killing Phaethon in the process.

THE MYTH OF NARCISSUS

A third story, very famous, that we know mainly through Ovid, is the story of Narcissus, a youth too proud to yield to any lover. Narcissus disdained those who loved him. As punishment for his excessive pride, Narcissus was made to fall in love with his own reflection in a pool.

Unable to leave the beauty of his reflection, Narcissus lost his will to live. He stared at his reflection until he starved to death. Narcissus is the origin of the term *narcissism*, self-love, or a fixation with oneself and one's physical appearance.

METAMORPHOSES — MOCK EPIC

The *Metamorphoses* is often called a mock epic. It's written in the same poetic meter — dactylic hexameter — found in traditional epics (*Iliad*, *Odyssey*, and *Aeneid*). However, we know from the first sentence of his work that Ovid is not writing a traditional epic. He states outright that he intends to create something new, and not to simply mimic Virgil's *Aeneid* or Homer's *Iliad*.

The one unifying theme of Ovid's stories is that they all involve transformations. Aside from that, the poem leaps from story to story, often with few or no connections among them. Ovid gathered his material from early Greek works but added his own twist to many of them.

Sometimes, a character from one story is connected to the next story. And sometimes the mythical characters themselves tell stories within stories. Ovid was not afraid to change details, if the change better suited his purpose. Sometimes the poem retells central events in the world of Greek and Roman myth. But at other times he wanders in apparently arbitrary directions.

Ovid's work is highly polished, very literary, and self-consciously ironic. Concerning any myth in the book, however, we can never assume that Ovid is giving us the straight version. Consider any story in *Metamorphoses*. Is it an authentic ancient Greek myth that Ovid has shared, more or less as Hesiod might have? Or, more likely, has this ancient story been altered, perhaps dramatically, to satisfy Ovid's literary impulses? Or, did the story spring, fully developed, out of Ovid's head?

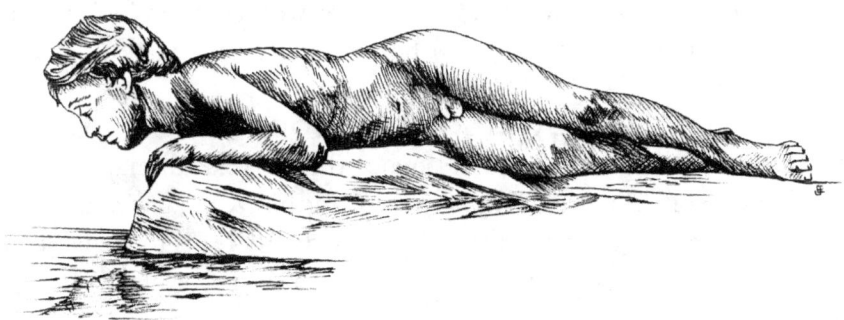

MYTH OF NARCISSUS. Narcissus disdained those who loved him. As punishment for his excessive pride, he was made to fall in love with his own reflection in a pool. Unable to leave the beauty of his face in the water, Narcissus lost his will to live. He stared at his reflection until he starved to death.

FROM SAVAGERY TO CIVILIZATION

PYRAMUS AND THISBE

Here's another example: The myth of Pyramus and Thisbe is the proto-Romeo and Juliet story. Two young lovers are forbidden by their parents to marry. They run away together. Pyramus thinks his beloved Thisbe is dead, and so he kills himself. Thisbe returns, finds Pyramus' body, and kills herself.

That's the short version. This story does not appear anywhere else in classical literature before Ovid. Ovid could very well have invented it. We don't know. Is the story of Pyramus and Thisbe an actual traditional myth? Or is it a nice little story that Ovid dreamt up and put into the book for his own reasons?

MAJOR THEME OF LOVE

The major recurring theme in all of Ovid's work is love (and especially the transformative power of love) – either personal love, or love personified in the figure of Cupid. But Ovid did not hold positive romantic notions of love. Rather, he viewed love as a dangerous, destabilizing force. In *Metamorphoses*, Ovid demonstrates how love has power over everyone, mortals and gods alike.

Most of Ovid's stories contain sexuality, sexual adventure, and frequently sexual perversion. Many are shocking. Throughout the poem, there runs the entire gamut of possible human emotions and interactions – from violent and grotesque stories to charming and attractive stories. Ovid includes stories of men in love with women, men in love with men, women in love with women, men in love with animals, women in love with their fathers, and even a man in love with a statue.

POWER OF THE GODS

The power of the gods is a second major theme. Like all major Greek and Roman epics, *Metamorphoses* emphasizes that *hubris*, or excessive pride, is a fatal flaw, which inevitably leads to a character's downfall. We just saw examples of this in the stories of Narcissus and Phaethon.

Hubris always attracts the notice and punishment of the gods. They disdain all human beings who attempt to place themselves at the level of the gods. Some, especially women like Niobe (Remember

Niobe's tears?), actively challenge the gods and goddesses to defend their prowess. Others display *hubris* by ignoring their own mortality. Ovid embraced the idea that people cannot escape their destiny. He also held that the concept of fate both supports and undermines the power of the gods. The gods may hold a longer term view of fate, but they are still subject to its dictates.

According to Ovid, *hubris* and fate, like love, are universal equalizers in a world of powerful gods. Nevertheless, he treats the ancient gods of classical mythology very humorously. Ovid makes fun of their anthropomorphic nature. The gods are often perplexed, humiliated and ridiculed by fate and Cupid. In particular, irrational love often confounds Apollo, the god of pure reason and moderation. The work as a whole inverts the accepted order. It elevates humans and human passions, while rendering the gods self-absorbed, vengeful, and objects of low humor.

REVENGE MOTIVATES TRANSFORMATIONS

Revenge, another major theme of *Metamorphoses*, often motivates whatever transformations the stories are explaining.

The gods avenge themselves and change mortals into birds or beasts just to prove their own superiority. Violence, and often rape, occur in almost every story. Ovid generally portrays women negatively, either as virginal girls fleeing from rape-minded gods, or as scorned women wielding the only tools available to their subjugated sex – malice and vengeance.

OVID THROUGH THE AGES

More than any other single person, Ovid is responsible for making Greek and Roman mythology accessible to readers over the 2000 years since he died. If that seems like an overstatement, consider what occurred in the intervening centuries.

Between the fourth century and 11th century AD, and later on during the early Middle Ages, Latin was the main language of communication in Western Europe. Literary evidence from these centuries is sparse. Most surviving literature is Christian-oriented and deals with church matters and the like.

In the late 11th century and onward, the high Middle Ages and Renaissance, classical literature, and particularly Ovid, came back into favor and greatly influenced European culture. *Metamorphoses* became an important text.

The growth of cathedral schools during this period raised awareness of Ovid's work. Classical literature, in general, survived mainly in the libraries of monasteries, convents, and great churches. Church scribes preserved classical literature by copying it laboriously by hand, manuscript to manuscript. Many works were lost, simply because the labor required to copy them was too great to justify, relative to their perceived importance. But primary classical works – Virgil, Ovid, the historian Livy, and a few others – were copied and continued to exist.

Ovid was more popular than Virgil or any other classical writer. Medieval writers interpreted *Metamorphoses* as a collection of allegories, both moral allegories in general and Christian allegories specifically. They were viewed as moral examples, to be interpreted and taught to the young. This new religious approach provided the book with staying power and broadened its influence.

By the 14th century, *Metamorphoses*, in Ovid's Latin original, was well known in England. English grammar school students learned Latin, that is, Latin grammar, and specifically Ovid's Latin grammar. And then in the year 1480, *Metamorphoses* was translated into English. That opened up the work to a large group of non-Latin-speaking readers.

OVID'S INFLUENCE BEYOND RECKONING

For English literature and culture, however, Ovid's influence on Shakespeare became the crucial point.

Shakespeare clearly knew *Metamorphoses* very well. It permeates his work to an extent that can hardly be exaggerated. It's almost as if Shakespeare had an open copy of *Metamorphoses* on hand as he wrote just about every page of just about every play.

When Shakespeare sought a point of comparison, or searched for the perfect metaphor or simile, one of Ovid's stories often sprang to his mind. Most people agree that Shakespeare's influence on English literature is great beyond reckoning. It's also true that Ovid's influence on English literature – through Shakespeare – is great beyond reckoning.

CLASSICAL MYTHOLOGY PERMEATES OUR CULTURE

Ovid is only one author, but his work can ably represent the enormous influence that classical mythology overall has had and continues to have on later Western civilization, both European and American. For centuries, authors have taken themes, images, plots, characters, and points of comparison from Homer, Virgil, the Greek tragedians, and many other classical authors, including Ovid. Writers who draw upon ancient authors by definition owe a debt to classical mythology. James Joyce named his novel *Ulysses*, signaling a reworking of the *Odyssey*. Eugene O'Neill's play, *Mourning Becomes Electra*, reworks the myth of the House of Atreus.

A more current example could be Charles Frazier's novel, *Cold Mountain*, which is set in the post-Civil War American South. The novel owes much of its plot, many of its specific episodes, and much of his imagery to the *Odyssey*.

So too do films, such as the Coen Brothers film with George Clooney, *Oh Brother, Where Art Thou?*, whose plot and images directly mimic the *Odyssey*. Another is the film *Troy*, starring Brad Pitt, which reimagines the *Iliad*. Brad Pitt, of course, plays Achilles. (*I saw* Troy, *and, unfortunately, was disappointed. That's because I knew Achilles when I was young. Achilles was a friend of mine. And, sadly, Brad Pitt is no Achilles.*)

And finally, if those examples are not sufficiently current, try this: An article that ran in the New Yorker magazine in 2018, "*Reading Ovid in the Age of the #MeToo Movement*," by Katy Waldman.

Classical mythology clearly permeates our culture.

OUR CLASSICAL LEGACY

According to many scholars, myth is important for deeper reasons than merely its influence on our culture. They say that myth taps into a deep structure or psychological tendency of the human mind.

Myth mediates binary opposites, they say, or it expresses our repressed desires, or it links the human psyche to archetypes.

Even if those interpretations are all correct, a question still arises. Why does *classical myth*, in particular, seem to fit our modern culture so well? Elizabeth Vandiver has asked that question and offers her own answer — that there exists a built-in understanding of classical myth in our culture. It resonates in a way the myths of other cultures do not.

In the stories of Greco-Roman antiquity, we inherit not just stories, but a whole cast of mind or worldview. That cast of mind may influence us more than we realize, even today. Certainly classical myths shaped the cultures that developed them – Greece and Rome. In the same way, classical myths have helped shape our culture.

These stories of classical mythology may indeed reflect archetypes, or patterns of human thought, that any culture of any time might embrace. But that's not why classical myths appeal to us.

The reason for their appeal lies in their familiarity. That familiarity comes from hearing the stories of classical myth repeated generation after generation for 2500 years. These 25 centuries of repetition have replicated story patterns in the textures of our minds.

We in our society, as people do in all societies, tell ourselves stories that encode our hopes, aspirations and fears. Many of the stories of our modern society preserve traces of classical culture and myth. They are part of our classical legacy.

CHAPTER XV
FINAL RECKONING

Wxx HAT SHOULD WE REMEMBER ABOUT THE REMARKABLE JOURNEY THE ANCIENT GREEKS UNDERTOOK, AND THE NATURE OF WHAT THEY ACHIEVED? Let me sum up.

In their early days, that is, during the Greek Bronze Age (3000-1000 BC), the Greeks were as savage and barbaric as any tribal culture we know of.

Thomas Hobbes, in *Leviathan*, said, *"Without written communication, without a system of social justice, and in continual fear and danger of violent death, the life of man would be solitary, poor, nasty, brutish and short."*

That nicely sums up life for Early Bronze Age Greeks, with emphasis on *"nasty, brutish and short."* For indeed the outlook was bleak for humankind in those early days. The human species was frail, despite their brave façades, facing as they did nearly inevitable extermination.

However, over 2500 years, from 3000 to 500 BC, the Greeks not only survived those perilous times, they prevailed. They created and re-created themselves. They grew in sophistication, understanding and wisdom. They eventually produced the world's first democracy. Suffering and hardship were the driving forces behind their journey. Their own blood marked each step of their way.

SIX MAJOR THEMES

As the ancient Greek people stumbled their way over the centuries from savagery to civilization, six major themes appear and reappear in their mythology and help explain how they did it. They are:

1. **The sustaining power of their creation myths** about the cosmos, gods, heroes and men;

2. **The dominance of fate** over every particular of their lives;

In the war with the titans, LIGHTNING-WIELDING ZEUS overcame his father Cronus and chained him and the other titans to the underground. Zeus then became supreme ruler of the gods.

3. The importance of carefully nurturing the lopsided relationship with their gods. They were suffering mortals who bore individual responsibility for their actions. They were pitted against nearly omnipotent, indifferent, and fickle gods who bore responsibility for nothing;

4. The danger of arrogance and excessive pride (*hubris*);

5. The development of a code of right behavior that guided men's actions in all times and circumstances – war and peace; and finally,

6. The gradual substitution of complex, comprehensive and institutional social justice (guilt-culture) **for individual revenge killing** (shame-culture).

THEME ONE: POWERFUL CREATION MYTHS

In their creation stories, the Greeks developed myths sufficiently powerful to sustain them in their harsh circumstances, explain their place of primacy on the planet, and propel them forward to a better world.

Hesiod's *Theogony* describes how the material universe, gods, demigods, heroes and men all came into being. The gods did not create the universe; they were part of it. The universe, and with it the primal gods, simply came into existence.

The gods, even Zeus, the supreme god, were not omnipotent. They were not transcendent, but they *were* immortal. They could not die for at least as long as the universe lasts. They were highly anthropomorphic: they ate, drank, slept, mated, and felt emotions, just as humans do.

In the beginning, Chaos somehow begot Gaia, mother earth; Tartarus, the great region beneath earth; and Eros, sexual desire. Gaia was at first shaped like a flat disc. She then molded herself into the Mediterranean Sea region familiar to the Greeks. Then, without help, Gaia gave birth to Uranus, the starry sky, who became a dome over her.

FROM SAVAGERY TO CIVILIZATION

Gaia mated with Uranus, her son, and together they bore the titans – the first generation of gods. Gaia then conspired with her son Cronus to overthrow Uranus and become ruler over all. During the rule of Cronus, the titans produced thousands of children, i.e., rivers, mountains, islands, and so forth, thereby populating the earth with all of its physical features.

Then erupted another dramatic takeover. Zeus overthrew and imprisoned his powerful father Cronus. He then banded together with his siblings. Together they made war against the titans and defeated them. Zeus and his siblings installed themselves as lords of the universe and settled atop Mount Olympus. From that day forward, the Olympians ruled, and Zeus was their king.

ZEUS' WILL TO POWER

The most notable feature of this creation myth is the drive from the very beginning for power and dominance. This is how Hesiod traced the gods themselves from savagery to a peak of absolute control. These gods not only succeeded prior generations, they suppressed them. Cronus suppressed his father, Uranus, by castrating him. Zeus suppressed his father, Cronus, by blasting him and the titans with lightning.

Zeus ruled on high because he was too strong for the law of retaliation. He felt neither shame nor guilt. His was the invincible masculine will to power. He was the father who triumphed over Mother Earth. His justice was the way of Might Makes Right. And when he began dealing with humans, he brought to bear that same unyielding attitude.

PROMETHEUS, MAN'S BEST FRIEND

The Greeks were a strong people. They proudly faced the severest challenges. And yet, it was clear during that very difficult beginning that, every now and then, humans could use a break. And finally, as told in one of Hesiod's creation myths, they did get a break, actually two breaks.

They came in the form of one, a gift, and two, an instructive example of behavior modeling. Both gifts came from a god,

Prometheus, man's best friend ever. With the aid of wise Prometheus, mankind could more easily survive his harsh environment. And the asymmetric relationship mankind had with the gods tilted a bit in mankind's favor.

Prometheus stole fire from the heavens and gave it to men. To compound this felony, Prometheus later showed how, sometimes, the gods can be tricked to man's benefit. He convinced Zeus to accept the worst parts of the animal that he received as a sacrifice from men.

Zeus was outraged at Prometheus' treachery. Prometheus had given humans fire and taught them how to cheat the gods. To punish Prometheus, Zeus chained him to a rock. Every day for eternity an eagle would fly in, eat his liver, and fly away.

Of course, Zeus was also angry with men, even though they had committed no crime. They had accepted help from Prometheus, and so Zeus chose to punish them as well. You recall the punishment. Zeus sent women to men to cause them eternal trouble. The first woman was Pandora.

Zeus was a vindictive god. He punished men for their own misdeeds, but also for the misdeeds of Prometheus. And so men's suffering and hardship continued unabated, as did the gods' capricious vindictiveness. But now, with the gifts from Prometheus, men gained a bit of an edge in their struggle for survival. They began to make progress.

THEME TWO: DOMINANCE OF FATE

One explanation for Hesiod's early pessimism about man's prospects may be the burden of fate that the Greeks believed every man and god carry. The inability of any mortal or immortal to change a prescribed outcome stemmed from the three Fates: sisters Clotho, who spins the thread of life; Lachesis, who assigns each person's destiny; and Atropos, who carries the scissors to snip the thread of life at its end.

These three divinities pervade all the stories of Greek myth. Nothing can be done to alter or prolong the destiny of one's life, regardless of the preparations or precautions taken.

FROM SAVAGERY TO CIVILIZATION

Throughout classical mythology, the workings of fate are the major concern of gods and humans alike. Even Zeus, ruler of the gods, is governed by the laws of fate – as both an agent and victim. Zeus was destined to overthrow his father, and he himself is fated to be overthrown by one who is not yet born.

Zeus himself cannot change one's ultimate fate. However, by interfering in interim steps, he can raise havoc with the process of reaching it.

In Homer's *Iliad*, the gods knew (although humans did not) that Troy was fated to lose the Trojan War. Zeus could not alter that fate. But he could and did meddle. At the request of Thetis, Achilles' mother, Zeus allowed the Trojans to win several victories over the Greeks on the day Achilles refused to fight. On that day, it appeared that the war was unfolding in Troy's favor.

THE AENEID: FATE AS RELIGIOUS PRINCIPLE

The dominance of fate was also a major theme of Virgil's *Aeneid*. To Virgil's Roman audience, fate was a divine, religious principle that determined the course of history and culminated in the Roman Empire. Fate preordained both the direction and destination of Aeneas' course on his journey to Italy. His suffering and glories in battle and at sea merely postponed this unchangeable destiny.

The power of fate in the *Aeneid* stood above the power of the gods. Fate was often associated with the will of Jupiter, the supreme Roman god, because Jupiter's will trumped the will of all others. Lesser gods may have interfered in Aeneas' life to advance their own interests, but they could not alter the overall outcome of events.

OEDIPUS' STRUGGLE WITH FATE AND FREE WILL

In stories throughout classical mythology, we commonly find characters who do everything in their power to block negative fates, and yet fall prey to them. In the universe creation myth, an early example, Uranus knew he was fated to be overthrown by his son Cronus. And yet, despite his efforts to circumvent this fate, he could not prevent it.

Perhaps the most harrowing example of the inevitability of a fated outcome can be found in Sophocles' *Oedipus the King*. The main topic of the play is the conflict between fate and free will. Oedipus and his blood parents, Laius and Jocasta, were all fated to do the things they did. Apollo's oracle said so. Laius would be murdered by his son. Jocasta would marry and bear children to her son. Oedipus would kill his father and marry his mother. These fated outcomes would absolutely take place.

And yet, the inexorable working out of these fated outcomes occurred precisely because the characters exercised their free will to try to avoid them. Although Oedipus, Laius, and Jocasta were fated to commit the deeds they committed, those deeds happened because they chose to commit them. The characters took the courses of action they took through their own free will.

Throughout the play, fate and free will interacted to bring about what had to occur. The plot of the play consisted not of the predicted actions. Those had occurred years and years before. Rather, the plot consisted of Oedipus' process of discovering that he had already fulfilled the prediction. And this discovery was entirely due to his actions.

THEME THREE: INDIVIDUAL RESPONSIBILITY

Now consider the concept of fate in light of individual responsibility. Even individuals who were fated to perform wrong actions or transgressions, as Oedipus was, even they were still held responsible for those actions. To the Greeks, individual motivations were of trivial importance; individual actions were everything.

Many myths of classical mythology can be viewed as manuals of morality and correct conduct. They offered examples of which behaviors would be rewarded and which punished, especially behavior involving the gods. Woe to mortals who infringed on the rights of the gods, however slightly or unintentionally. They often suffered terrible punishments. We've seen several examples:

- Recall the hunter, Actaeon, who accidentally saw Artemis, goddess of the hunt, bathing nude. She punished him by having his hunting dogs rip him apart.

- Or the human Anchises, who slept with Aphrodite, goddess of love. Their child was the epic hero Aeneas. Anchises knew that men who mate with goddesses commit a great sin. However, he had not known beforehand that she was a goddess, so he survived the affair. Later, against the goddess' instructions, he boasted about it. He was lamed as a result.

- Or Penthius, king of Thebes, who refused to believe that his cousin Dionysus, god of wine, was actually a god. The god's women followers tore Penthius limb from limb.

- Or Paris, who abducted Helen, thus setting off the Trojan War. Paris was not absolved of his crushing guilt for violating *xenia* and stealing his host's wife. Moreover, his Trojan society was not absolved of his guilt either. Troy suffered terrible repercussions because of Paris's crime, despite the fact that Aphrodite told him to commit it.

- Or Agamemnon, who killed the sacred deer of Artemis and then boasted that he was a better hunter than the goddess. To her, this was a clear case of *hubris*. She retaliated by preventing the Greek ships from sailing to Troy. She demanded the sacrifice of Agamemnon's daughter, Iphigenia, to atone for his foolish boasting. Which he did. Which was the worst thing a father could possibly do. Agamemnon was replete with unabsolved guilt. Ten years later, enter Clytemnestra with an ax.

- Or the dozens of suitors of Penelope in Odysseus' Ithaca home in the *Odyssey*. Odysseus had been gone 20 years. In a severe violation of *xenia*, the suitors turned his home into a daily party, feasting and drinking at the host's expense. Each one hoped to marry Penelope and become king. Finally, Odysseus returned. Almost entirely by himself, he slaughtered them all.

FINAL RECKONING

In all of these connected stories, we see the complex interaction between the gods' commands and individual responsibility. Obeying the command of a god did not absolve the individual of responsibility. Humans were held to account for their actions.

THEME FOUR: DANGER OF HUBRIS

In its ancient Greek context, *hubris* described a personal quality of extreme or foolish pride, dangerous overconfidence, and arrogance. Hubristic behavior defied the norms of behavior or challenged the gods. In turn, it brought about the downfall of the perpetrator. *Hubris* often indicated a loss of contact with reality and an overestimation of one's own competence, accomplishments or capabilities. Many examples of hubristic behavior populate the stories of classical mythology. Here are three:

MYTH OF PHAETHON

Mainly from Ovid comes the story of Phaethon, who was the son of Apollo and a mortal woman.

Phaethon wondered whether the sun god really was his father. So he asked him, "*If you truly are my father, promise on the River Styx that you will grant me my one request.*"

Apollo made the promise. Phaethon's one request was to drive the chariot of the sun across the sky for one whole day. Apollo knew that such an attempt would be fatal, but he couldn't break his promise. He let the boy drive the chariot. But Phaethon couldn't control the horses. His dangerous incompetence put the entire earth at risk of burning up. To prevent this disaster, Zeus struck down the chariot with a thunderbolt. Phaethon was killed in the process.

MYTH OF NARCISSUS

Another is the story of Narcissus, a youth who was too proud to yield to any lover. Narcissus disdained all who loved him. As punishment for his foolish pride and overestimation of his own beauty, Narcissus was made to fall in love with his own reflection in a pool. Unable to leave the beauty of his reflection, Narcissus lost his will to live. He stared at his reflection until he starved to death, brought down by *hubris*.

FROM SAVAGERY TO CIVILIZATION

MYTH OF NIOBE'S TEARS

The third example is perhaps the most harrowing – the myth of Niobe and her 14 children. Carved on Apollo's temple at Delphi were two sayings that almost amounted to commandments. They were:

Know Yourself
Nothing in Excess

Know Yourself means to remember what kind of creature you are. Remember your limitations. Remember above all else that you are not a god. If you forget what kind of a creature you are, or if you have anything in excess, you risk offending the gods. In particular, humans must avoid *hubris*, which leads a person to claim more than his or her due.

It was very important to obey Apollo's maxims and avoid the dangers of *hubris*, but Niobe, queen of Thebes, apparently had not learned this lesson. She boasted of being better than the goddess Leto because Leto had fewer children. And so Apollo and Artemis, Leto's two divine children, killed all 14 of Niobe's human children. Niobe's big mistake was that she did not know herself. She forgot that her 14 children were human; Leto's two children were gods. Niobe's 14 children became 14 corpses because of Niobe's *hubris*.

These two maxims, *Know Yourself* and *Nothing in Excess*, work together. Niobe failed to know herself because she had so many live children that she thought she was safe and not liable to normal human experience. That was her great error. Apollo, as the god of reason and moderation, warns us that we should have nothing in excess. We should always practice moderation.

THEME FIVE: HONOR CODE OF GREEK HEROES

The fifth major theme permeating Greek culture was their code of honor, which guided their behavior in all circumstances for centuries. Hesiod described the early days of humankind. He told stories of mysterious, angry and capricious gods harrying humankind with onerous hardships. These stories accurately reflected the actuality of these people's lives.

They did indeed grind out a subsistence existence in a daily struggle to survive. They were burdened with a fate they could not escape or affect. Every day, they confronted their inevitable mortality. Then they died, usually at a young age.

Confronting our inevitable mortality is the human condition – at its essence no different today than during the Bronze Age. Understanding and coming to terms with the human condition lie at the heart of what it means to be human.

From the start, men have faced life's deepest challenges in harsh environments. The ancient Greeks must have asked themselves, as self-examining humans have done since: Must I die, really? If I must die, how should I live? How should I confront a certain death? After my death, will anyone remember who I was and what I achieved?

Their myths tell us how the ancient Greeks addressed these questions. Millennia ago, Prometheus stole fire for man and modeled behavior illustrating how to outwit the gods. With these hugely advantageous gifts, men could imagine a better future for themselves. And so they began developing, and orally transmitting down the generations, an unwritten guidebook of proper behavior, or code of honor. They believed that a people adhering to such a code could one day expect a better life.

This guide governed how a man, throughout his life, should behave, whether in peace or at war. It taught him how he should conduct himself on the battlefield; how he should interact with his family and community and keep his promises; how he should fulfill his responsibility to the assembly; and how he should behave in accordance with the strictures of *xenia*. This guide reached its apotheosis as the heroic code of honor that Homer's characters lived by.

THEME SIX: FROM SHAME-CULTURE TO GUILT-CULTURE

However, no overall system of social justice existed during those early times. In order to achieve social justice, the code of honor, by necessity, included revenge killing.

Revenge killing was a very effective tool. In the case of a murder, the victim's family would curse the offender and the offender's heirs with endless acts of violence. If the victim's family failed to seek appropriate retribution, the family would be shamed.

FROM SAVAGERY TO CIVILIZATION

This continual wreaking of personal justice represented proper law — blood for blood. Thus shame-culture, as it was called, helped achieve right and orderly social relations in barbaric societies for thousands of years.

However, the practice of achieving proper behavior through revenge justice gradually degenerated. Over time, it became little more than individual or family internecine warfare.

Recalling the dim past was often the only way to explain a required revenge killing of the moment. Avenging that dimly remembered crime seemed to call for acts of reckless blood vengeance forever into the future. In a culture aspiring to greatness, this was an unsustainable model for achieving right and orderly social relations. And that brings us to our sixth major theme — the substitution of institutional social justice for individual revenge justice.

FEATURES OF SHAME-CULTURE

Shame-culture applied not only to revenge justice for serious crimes but to any offense or slight against a man's honor. In a shame-culture, an individual placed high emphasis on preserving his honor. He should never allow himself to be publicly disgraced, as Achilles was at the hands of Agamemnon at Troy. People conformed to societal norms by seeking vengeance on a par with what they had suffered. Failure to do so meant shame or public dishonor.

To leave behind the barbarism inherent in a shame-culture and to achieve a higher level of civilization, the Greeks needed to make further progress in achieving right and orderly social relations.

To accomplish that, the notion of what constitutes right behavior had to change. The Greeks had to set aside, as no longer fitting, the traditional way of the tribal blood vendetta. The new order for ensuring civilized social justice must be determined by guilt for violating a law. Society, not the force of personal vengeance, must establish and enforce the law. Enter the guilt-culture.

FEATURES OF GUILT-CULTURE

In a guilt-culture, the individual, through his own will, internalizes and conforms to a moral code. He forces morality on himself and avoids violating society's condoned behaviors. And if he does become guilty of violating society's laws, he submits himself to a judgment and punishment that society, not the individual, deems appropriate.

Consider the transformation of Achilles in Homer's *Iliad*. After rejecting the ethos on which the Homeric code of honor was based, this revenge-seeking brute hit bottom. His entire history had perfectly exemplified the shame-culture at work.

Then, after wondering at Priam's face wet with tears, and tasting his own, Achilles reemerged as something approaching human. He began to dial up his own previously unrecognizable internal moral code – from zero to empathetic, from unashamed to guilty. Perhaps this was the first crack in the Greeks' monolithic shame-culture that had existed since the times Hesiod pessimistically wrote about.

FROM SAVAGERY TO CIVILIZATION

Transitioning an entire people from a shame-culture to a guilt-culture was a monumental undertaking. The Greeks slouched toward higher levels of civilization in fits and starts over thousands of years. How could they possibly do it, even with the help of Prometheus' gift of fire?

We find the answer in the *Oresteia* of Aeschylus, along with the earlier myths of Homer and Hesiod all the way back to the earliest divine rulers — Uranus, Cronus, and Zeus. These help us understand how Greece transitioned from barbaric tribalism to a highly sophisticated civilization.

The myths themselves describe tribal rites of passage. The *Oresteia* was the culmination of all the rite-of-passage and honor code-related stories that had come before it. Painful rites of initiation, suffering and death, followed by atonement and resurrection to a higher plane – that was the common tribal rite of passage required to immortalize a Greek hero.

What was needed ultimately was a cultural rite of passage that would carry Greek culture itself to a higher plane of civilization. They found that cultural rite of passage — from shame-culture to guilt-culture — in the *Oresteia*. It revolutionized the ancient world.

In conclusion, then, we celebrate the passage of Greek culture from savagery to civilization. We celebrate, as the critic Richard

Lattimore described it, "*Its grand centuries-long emergence from the darkness to the light, from the tribe to the aristocracy, to the democratic state.*"

And in that process, in the words of Robert Fagles, "*Aeschylus celebrates man's capacity for suffering, his courage to endure hereditary guilt and ethical conflicts, his battle for freedom and self-determination in the teeth of fate, and his strenuous collaboration with his gods to create a better world.*"

Nietzsche wrote of the ancient Greeks: "*What suffering this race must have endured, in order to create such beauty.*"

ATHENA PRESIDED OVER THE TRIAL OF ORESTES to find a just answer to the question of his guilt or innocence in the murder of his mother Clytemnestra. The cultural response of thousands of years was to avenge an alleged crime. Not this time. This was the first example of proper litigation and civilized decision-making. Athena created a blueprint for handling future revenge-killings.

BIBLIOGRAPHY

PRIMARY SOURCES

Aeschylus. *Agamemnon, Libation Bearers,* and *Eumenides.* Translated with introduction by Robert Fagles and W.B. Stanford. 1975.

Apollodorus. *The Library of Greek Mythology.* Translated by Robin Hard. 1997.

Euripides I. *Alcestis, Medea, Hippolytus,* and *The Heracleidae.* Translated with introduction by Richard Lattimore. 1955.

Herodotus. *The Histories.* Robert B. Strassler, Ed. *The Landmark Herodotus.* Translated by Andrea L. Purvis. Introduction by Rosalind Thomas. Pantheon Books. New York. 2007.

Hesiod. *Theogony* and *Works and Days.* Translated by M.L. West. 1988.

Homer. *The Iliad* (1990) and *The Odyssey* (1996). Translated by Robert Fagles. Introductions by Bernard Knox.

Livy. *The Early History of Rome.* Translated by Aubrey de Selincourt. 1960.

Ovid. *Metamorphoses.* Translated by Rolfe Humphries. 1955.

Sophocles. *The Three Theban Plays: Oedipus the King, Oedipus at Colonus,* and *Antigone.* Translated and introductions by Robert Fagles. 1982. 1960.

Virgil. *The Aeneid.* Translated by Robert Fagles. Introduction by Bernard Knox. 2008.

MODERN SOURCES

Hamilton, Edith. *The Greek Way.* W.W. Norton and Co. New York and London. 1930.

Hansen, William. *Classical Mythology: A Guide to the Mythical World of the Greeks and Romans.* Oxford University Press. New York. 2004.

Kirk, G.S. *The Nature of Greek Myths*. Penguin Books. London. 1974.

Michelakis, Pantelis. *Euripides: Iphigenia at Aulis*. Gerard Duckworth & Co. 2006.

Nagy, Gregory. *The Ancient Greek Hero in 24 Hours*. Harvard University Press. 2013.

Nagy, Gregory. *The Best of the Achaeans: Concepts of the Hero in Archaic Greek Poetry*. John Hopkins University Press. 1979, 1999.

Otto, Walter F. *Dionysus: Myth and Cult*. Indiana University Press. 1995.

Parkes, Henry Bamford. *Gods and Men: The Origins of Western Culture*. Alfred A. Knopf. New York. 1959.

Vandiver, Elizabeth. *Classical Mythology*. The Teaching Company: The Great Courses. Chantilly, Virginia. 2000.

Weigel, James. *Cliffs Notes on Mythology*. Wiley Publishing. New York. 1973.

GLOSSARY OF CHARACTERS

A

Achilles – Greatest warrior in the Greek army during the Trojan War and main protagonist of Homer's *Iliad*. Son of human Peleus and sea goddess Thetis.

Actaeon – While hunting, Actaeon espied the goddess Artemis naked while bathing. As punishment, she transformed him into a stag, and his own hunting dogs tore him apart.

Aegeus – Father of Theseus and king of Athens. In despair, threw himself off a cliff into the sea after seeing the wrong signaling flag from Theseus' returning ship. Theseus had neglected to change it. Source name for the Aegean Sea.

Aegisthus – In the *Oresteia*, son of Thyestes and nephew of Agamemnon of the House of Atreus. Sought revenge for the treatment by Atreus, Agamemnon's father, of Thyestes and his young sons. Also aspired to gain the throne. Became a lover of and co-conspirator with Agamemnon's wife Clytemnestra, as well as abettor in Agamemnon's murder. Killed by Orestes.

Aeneas – Trojan prince who led his people to Latium (Italy) after the fall of Troy. There he founded Roman civilization. Main protagonist in Virgil's *Aeneid*. Son of human Anchises and the goddess Venus.

Aeolus – In the *Odyssey*, god of the wind. He helped Odysseus once, but not twice, on the hero's long journey from Troy to his home in Ithaca.

Aerope – Wife of Atreus and mother of Agamemnon and Menelaus. After Atreus' brother Thyestes seduced her, she gave him a golden fleece which he incorrectly thought he would gain the throne.

Aeschylus – Greek tragic playwright (525-456 BC). Seven extant plays, including the *Oresteia* trilogy.

Aethra – Mother of the Greek hero Theseus.

Agamemnon – King of Mycenae. Father of Orestes, Electra, Chrysomethis, and Iphigenia, whom he sacrificed. Husband of Clytemnestra, who murdered him. Commander of the Greek forces in the Trojan War.

Ajax – In the *Iliad*, Greek warrior known for brute strength. During the sack of Troy, he raped Cassandra, daughter of King Priam, inside the supposedly safe temple of Athena.

Alcinous – In the *Odyssey*, king of the Phaeacians and father of Nausicaa. He welcomed Odysseus, who had washed up on his shore, listened to his story, and provided a ship to take him to Ithaca.

Alcmene – Mother of Heracles, the Greeks' Pan-Hellenic hero.

Amata – Wife of Latinus, king of Latium.

Anchises – Father of Aeneas. Lamed by Aphrodite for blabbing about their night of sex.

Andromache – In the *Iliad*, wife of Trojan hero Hector, and mother of infant boy Astyanax. She was sold into slavery when Troy fell.

Antigone – Daughter of Oedipus. Sister of Eteocles, Ismene and Polynices, whom she insisted on burying. Protagonist of eponymous play. Died for her beliefs. Also appeared in *Oedipus at Colonus*.

Antinous – In the *Odyssey*, leader of the suitors. He threatened Odysseus' household, his marriage to Penelope, and the rights of his son Telemachus – all in an effort to become ruler of Ithaca. Antinous was the first suitor Odysseus killed.

Aphrodite – Greek goddess of love and sexual desire. Roman Venus. Mother of Aeneas. Also a patron of Paris and fought on the Trojan side.

Apollo – Son of Zeus and Leto. God of prophecy from his oracle at Delphi. Also the god of the sun, music, light and poetry, as well as reason and moderation. He fought on the Trojan side in the *Iliad*. Twin brother of Artemis; both were archers.

GLOSSARY OF CHARACTERS

Apollodorus — Called Pseudo-Apollodorus. So many authors with that name wrote around AD 100. Don't know which one wrote *The Library of Greek Mythology*.

Ares – Son of Zeus and Hera. Greek god of war. Known for his brutality and cruel nature; also a coward. Roman Mars, where he was more highly regarded than Jupiter, ruler of the gods.

Argus – Odysseus' ancient dog. He recognized his master, who had been gone for 20 years, and then died.

Ariadne – Daughter of King Minos of Crete, keeper of the monster Minotaur in an impenetrable labyrinth. She loved Theseus, so she helped him. With the aid of a ball of yarn (Clue of Ariadne), Theseus found and slew the beast and then safely escaped. He later abandoned Ariadne.

Artemis – Daughter of Zeus and Leto. Goddess of hunting, chastity and wildness. Roman Diana. Twin sister of fellow archer Apollo. Forced Agamemnon to sacrifice his daughter Iphigenia to atone for a mild offense.

Ascanius – Young son of Aeneas and Creusa.

Astyanax — Infant son of Trojan hero Hector and Andromache. Thrown from the walls of Troy by the Greek warrior Neoptolemos, son of Achilles.

Athena – Daughter of Zeus and Metis. Goddess of wisdom and just war, also reason and purity. Roman Minerva. The form of her birth was unusual – springing full grown and battle-ready from the head of Zeus. Fought for the Greeks in the Trojan War. Supported Odysseus on his way home to Ithaca in the *Odyssey*. Introduced a new form of social justice in the *Oresteia*.

Atreus – King of Mycenae. Son of Pelops and Hippodameia. Forced his brother Thyestes into cannibalism by inviting him to a banquet and feeding him his own two young sons.

Atropos – Third of the three Fates. She carried the scissors to snip the thread of life at its end.

Augean Stables – Heracles flushed out these stables by diverting two rivers through them. It was the fifth of his 12 labors.

FROM SAVAGERY TO CIVILIZATION

B-C

Bacchus – See Dionysus.

Briseis – In the *Iliad*, slave girl captured by the Greek army and awarded to Achilles. He was forced to turn her over to Agamemnon.

Calchas – Greek army's resident prophet and soothsayer at Troy.

Calypso – Sea nymph who kept Odysseus on her island Ogygia for seven years. She hoped to make him her husband and promised to make him immortal. Odysseus demurred and was finally released.

Cassandra – Daughter of Trojan King Priam and Hecuba. A prophetess who became Agamemnon's war prize. She was murdered by Clytemnestra, Agamemnon's wife, when the pair returned to Mycenae.

Cerberus – Three-headed dog that guarded the entrance to Hades. Heracles captured Cerberus in the final of his 12 labors.

Ceres – See Demeter.

Cerynian Hind – Golden-horned deer sacred to Artemis. Heracles captured it in the third of his 12 labors.

Chaos – In the beginning, the one primordial entity – empty void, not a state of disorder.

Charybdis — In the *Odyssey* and *Aeneid*, a whirlpool-creating monster living on one side of a narrow channel of water, opposite her counterpart Scylla.

Chryseis – In the *Iliad*, slave girl captured by the Greek army and awarded to Agamemnon. He refused to give her up when her father Chryses pled and offered generous terms.

Chryses – Father of Chryseis. Prays to Apollo who brought down a plague on the Greek camp for Agamemnon's violation of honorable behavior.

Circe – Beautiful enchantress on the island of Aeaea, where Odysseus landed. She transformed his men into pigs but later lifted the spell. The two became lovers, he and his men stayed a year, and she aided in their final departure.

GLOSSARY OF CHARACTERS

Clotho – First of the three Fates, Clotho spun the thread of life.

Clytemnestra – In the *Oresteia*, wife of Agamemnon, whom she murdered, because he had sacrificed their daughter Iphigenia. Also the mother of Electra, Orestes, and Chrysomethis. Orestes slew Clytemnestra for the death of their father. She harried the Furies to wreak revenge on Orestes for his matricide.

Creon – King of Thebes in *Antigone*. Creon violated divine laws, and his wife and son died. Also appeared in *Oedipus the King*.

Cretan Bull – Heracles' seventh of 12 labors was to capture this bull and bring it home.

Creusa – Wife of Aeneas. She died trying to escape falling Troy.

Cronus – Son of Gaia, mother earth, and Uranus, the sky. Cronus conspired with Gaia to castrate and neutralize Uranus. Under Cronus' rule, Gaia's children, the titans, were free to be born.

Cupid – In Roman mythology, a god in the form of a winged child, who shot arrows of love. Greek Eros.

D-E

Daphne – Nymph and daughter of a river god. Apollo pursued her, but she ran away. She sought help from her father, who transformed her into a laurel tree. Apollo then made the laurel his sacred tree.

Dardanus – Son of Zeus and founder of Troy.

Deianira — Second wife of Greek hero Heracles. She gifted him a poisoned robe that nearly killed him.

Demeter – Goddess of grain and agriculture. Roman Ceres. Mother of Persephone, queen of the underworld. Known as the goddess who continually sorrows.

Diana – See Artemis.

Dido – In the *Aeneid*, queen of Carthage. "Married" to Aeneas. Committed suicide when he left for Italy.

Dionysus – Son of Zeus and human Semele. Roman Bacchus. God of wine. Tragic world view: Everything always has its opposite in itself. Also patron god of theater.

Electra – In *Libation Bearers*, daughter of Agamemnon and Clytemnestra. Sister of Iphigenia, Orestes, and Chrysomethis. Unindicted co-conspirator in Orestes' murder of their mother.

Epimetheus – Titan brother of Prometheus. Botched his part of the effort to create humans.

Eramanthian Boar – Heracles brought this beast back to Eurystheus in the fourth of his 12 labors.

Erato – Muse of poetry, whom Virgil invoked in the *Aeneid*.

Eris – Goddess of strife and discord. Rolled out a golden apple with the words, *For the Fairest,* at the wedding of Peleus and Thetis. Strife and discord ensued.

Eros – Sexual desire and one of four primary deities. Later a winged child who shot arrows of love. Roman Cupid.

Eteocles – Son of Oedipus. Brother of Polynices, Ismene and Antigone. He and his brother Polynices slew each other in battle before *Antigone* opened.

Eumenides – Kindly Ones, sometimes the terrible Furies. They ruled over unavenged crimes, especially within families.

Euripides – Greek tragic playwright (480-406 BC). Wrote more than 90 plays; only 18 extant.

Eurycleia – Odysseus' old nurse, who recognized him upon his return.

GLOSSARY OF CHARACTERS

Eurydice – Wife of King Creon in *Antigone*. On hearing of her son Haemon's death, she cursed Creon and killed herself.

Eurymachus – Second most important suitor hungering for Odysseus' wife and throne in the *Odyssey*.

Eurystheus – Heracles' cousin and recipient of everything Heracles brought back from his 12 labors.

Evander – In the *Aeneid*, king of Pallantium, site of future Rome. Aeneas' ally in the war against Turnus' forces.

F-G-H

Fates – Three immortal sisters who, independent of Zeus, prescribed an unchangeable destiny for gods and men.

Gaia – Mother earth and one of four primary deities.

Ganymede – Young Trojan prince abducted by Zeus to be his paramour and cup-bearer.

Geryon – Triple-bodied monster with a herd of cattle. In Heracles' tenth labor, he defeated Geryon and stole his cattle.

Hades – Ruler, along with his wife Persephone, of the dead.

Haemon – In *Antigone*, son of King Creon. Betrothed to Antigone, he committed suicide when she was condemned to die.

Hector – In the *Iliad*, greatest Trojan warrior and commander of the Trojan forces. Son of King Priam and Hecuba, and brother of Paris. Slain on the battlefield by the Greek warrior Achilles.

Hecuba – Wife of King Priam and queen of Troy. Mother of Hector and Paris.

Helen – Daughter of Zeus and human Leda. Wife of Menelaus, king of Sparta. Kidnapped by Paris and carried off to Troy. War ensued.

Helenus – In the *Aeneid*, son of Priam with the gift of prophecy. Advised Aeneas.

Hephaestus – Blacksmith of the gods. Roman Vulcan.

Hera – Wife and sister of Zeus. Goddess of married love. Roman Juno. In the *Iliad*, Hera avidly supported the Greeks, despised Trojans. In the *Aeneid*, Juno was Trojan Aeneas' greatest opposition on his way to Italy.

Heracles – Son of Zeus and human Alcmene. Pan-Hellenic hero of Greece. Roman Hercules. Completed 12 labors to atone for his crimes. His body died on a funeral pyre, but his spirit became immortal. The human hero who suffered, died and became a god.

Hermes – Messenger of the gods. Roman Mercury.

Herodotus – Greek historian (484-425 BC). Father of History. Published *The Histories* about the Greco-Persian Wars in 440 BC.

Hesiod – Ancient Greek poet (ca 750-650 BC). Wrote about Greek mythology, inter alia, in *Theogony* and *Works and Days*.

Hesperides – Three goddesses, daughters of Night, had a dragon-guarded tree that blossomed with golden apples. Heracles, in his 11th labor, stole their apples.

Hestia – Goddess of the hearth. Roman Vesta.

Hippodameia – Wife of Pelops of the House of Atreus.

Hippolyta – Amazon queen. In his ninth labor, Heracles fought her and forcibly removed the Belt of Hippolyta.

Homer – Ancient Greek epic poet (ca 800-700 BC). Author of the *Iliad* and the *Odyssey*.

I-J-K-L

Iphigenia – Daughter of Clytemnestra and Agamemnon, who sacrificed her to appease the goddess Artemis. Sister of Orestes, Electra, and Chrysomethis.

GLOSSARY OF CHARACTERS

Ismene – Daughter of Oedipus and sister of Antigone, Polynices and Eteocles. Appeared in *Oedipus at Colonus* and *Antigone.*

Janus – Roman divinity usually portrayed as having two faces that looked in opposite directions.

Jason – Greek hero who sailed his ship, the Argo, with wife Medea in search of the Golden Fleece.

Jocasta – In *Oedipus the King*, past wife of King Laius and queen of Thebes. Unknowingly married her biological son, Oedipus, and bore him four children — years before the play opens.

Jove – See Zeus.

Juno – See Hera.

Jupiter – See Zeus.

Lachesis – Second of the three Fates. She assigned each person's destiny.

Laertes – Father of Odysseus.

Laius – In *Oedipus the King*, Laius was the king of Thebes and biological father of Oedipus, who had unknowingly killed him long before the play opens.

Latinus – In the *Aeneid*, king of Latium and husband of Amata. Supported Aeneas' efforts to settle there.

Lavinia – In the *Aeneid*, daughter of King Latinus and Amata. Would one day marry Aeneas.

Leda – Human woman ravished by Zeus, who arrived in the form of a wild swan. Their coupling produced Helen, the most beautiful woman in the world.

Lernaean Hydra – Snake with nine heads, one of which was immortal. Heracles vanquished it in the second of his 12 labors.

Leto – Fifth wife of Zeus and mother of Apollo and Artemis.

Livy – Roman historian (64-17 BC). Published *The History of Rome* in 32 BC.

M-N-O

Mares of Diomedes – As his eighth of 12 labors, Heracles tamed these man-eating mares and fed Diomedes to them.

Mars – See Ares.

Menelaus – In the *Iliad*, king of Sparta. Brother of Agamemnon. Husband of Helen.

Mercury – See Hermes.

Merope – In *Oedipus the King*, queen of Corinth and wife of King Polybus. Raised Oedipus from infancy.

Minerva – See Athena.

Minotaur – Man-eating monster with head of a bull and body of a man. Killed by Theseus.

Muses – Nine nymphs of the arts.

Myrtilos – In the myth of the House of Atreus, he was a slave charioteer who helped Pelops win the hand of Hippodameia, by arranging for the death of her father. Pelops later threw Myrtilos off a cliff.

Narcissus – Youth too proud to yield to any lover. As punishment, made to fall in love with his own image in a pool. Stared at his reflection until he starved to death.

Nausicaa – Daughter of King Alcinous of Phaeacia. She discovered Odysseus washed up on their shores.

Nemean Lion — Heracles clubbed this beast to death in the first of his 12 labors. He took the lion's skin for his cloak.

Neoptolemos – In the *Iliad*, a Greek warrior. Son of Achilles. Killed Astyanax and King Priam. Pyrrhus to the Romans.

Neptune – See Poseidon.

GLOSSARY OF CHARACTERS

Nestor – In the *Iliad*, oldest Greek warrior at Troy.

Niobe – Human mother who claimed she was more worthy of worship than the goddess Leto, because she had 14 children, while Leto only had two. Leto's two children – the divine Apollo and Artemis – killed all 14 of her children with arrows.

Nobody – In the *Odyssey*, the name Odysseus assumed in order to free himself and his men from the Cyclops Polyphemus.

Odysseus – Hero of the *Odyssey*, which related his trials and adventures in his 10-year journey from Troy to Ithaca. Known as a champion of heroic intelligence. Also appeared in the *Iliad*.

Oedipus – King of Thebes who slowly discovered that long ago he had unknowingly murdered his father, married his mother, and with her begot four children. He blinded and exiled himself.

Orestes – Son of Agamemnon and Clytemnestra, whom he murdered to avenge his father's death at her hands. In the first example of proper litigation, Athena presided over a trial that acquitted Orestes of the crime of matricide.

Ovid – Roman poet (43 BC–18 AD). In AD 8, published *Metamorphoses*, a work with 15 books and 250 myths. Related stories of transformations in Greek and Roman mythology.

P-Q

Palinurus – In the *Aeneid*, steersman on Aeneas' ship. The god Neptune required a sacrifice before Aeneas could safely cross the sea and enter the Land of the Dead, so Aeneas sacrificed Palinurus.

Pandora – First woman. Opened Pandora's jar, releasing all the evils of the world, except hope.

Paris – Trojan prince who kidnapped Helen and carried her off to Troy. In the war that followed, he acted cowardly. Slew Achilles with an arrow to his heel.

Patroclus – In the *Iliad,* close friend of Achilles. Fought in Achilles' place and was killed by Hector.

Peleus – Father of Achilles and husband of the sea nymph Thetis.

Pelops – In the myth of the House of Atreus, son of Tantalus. As a child, he was murdered by Tantalus and offered as food to the gods. They refused, punished Tantalus, and restored Pelops' body. As an adult, Pelops helped cause the death of his father-in-law. He shoved Myrtilos, the slave charioteer, off a cliff.

Penelope – Wife of Odysseus, queen of Ithaca, and mother of Telemachus. She waited 20 years for Odysseus' return from the war.

Penthius – King of Thebes and cousin of Dionysus. He didn't believe Dionysus was a god. Dionysus' followers destroyed him.

Persephone – Wife of Hades and queen of the dead. Daughter of Demeter. Roman Proserpina. Known as the goddess who repeatedly died.

Perseus – Legendary founder of Mycenae. Greatest Greek hero and slayer of monsters before Heracles. Famously slew the gorgon Medusa.

Phaethon – Son of Apollo. At Phaethon's persistent request, Apollo allowed him to drive the chariot of the sun across the sky for one day. Disaster followed, and he was destroyed.

Pindar – Ancient Greek lyric poet (522-443 BC).

Plutarch – Greek biographer and essayist (AD 46 -120). In AD 110, published *Plutarch's Lives*, a series of biographies of famous Greeks and Romans.

Polexena – Daughter of King Priam. At the end of the Trojan War, she was slaughtered on the grave of Achilles.

Polybus – In the myth of the House of Oedipus, he was king of Corinth. He and his wife Queen Merope became Oedipus' de facto parents and raised him from infancy.

GLOSSARY OF CHARACTERS

Polynices – Son of Oedipus. Brother of Antigone, Ismene and Eteocles. Appeared alive in *Oedipus at Colonus*, and dead but unburied in *Antigone*. He and Eteocles slew each other in battle.

Polyphemus – Cyclops whose one eye Odysseus poked out. Ate several of Odysseus' men.

Poseidon – Brother of Zeus and god of the sea. Roman Neptune. Odysseus' primary divine opponent on his journey home.

Priam – In the *Iliad*, king of Troy and husband of Hecuba. Father of Hector and Paris inter alia. Priam wept as he clasped the knees of his enemy Achilles. Pled for the body of his son Hector, whom Achilles had killed in battle and then defiled.

Procrustes – In the myth of the Athenian hero Theseus, Procrustes was a rogue smith and bandit, who tortured and murdered travelers on their way to Athens. Theseus tortured and killed him, using Procrustes' own methods.

Prometheus – Man's best friend. In one of Hesiod's creation myths, a titan god who gifted men fire stolen from the gods. Taught men how to outwit the gods.

Proserpina – See Persephone.

Pyramus and Thisbe – Proto-Romeo and Juliet story that appeared in Ovid's *Metamorphoses*.

Pyrrhus – See Neoptolemus.

R-S

Remus – In Roman mythology, son of the god Mars and Rhea Silvia, descendant of Aeneas. Twin brother of Romulus, who murdered him.

Rhea – Titan goddess wife of Cronus. Mother of Zeus.

Rhea Silvia – In Roman mythology, descendant of Aeneas and mother of Romulus and Remus.

Romulus – In Roman mythology, son of the god Mars and Rhea Silvia, descendant of Aeneas. Founder of Rome. Twin brother of Remus, whom he murdered.

Sappho – Ancient Greek poet from the island of Lesbos (ca 630—570 BC).

Scylla – In the *Odyssey* and *Aeneid*, six-headed monster living on one side of a narrow channel of water, opposite her counterpart Charybdis.

Semele – Mother of the god Dionysus, whom she bore twice.

Sibyl – In the *Aeneid*, priestess of the oracle at Cumae. She guided Aeneas on his visit to the underworld.

Sirens – In the *Odyssey* and *Aeneid*, creatures who lured nearby sailors with enchanting music and singing voices to shipwreck on the rocky coast of their island.

Sophocles – Greek tragic playwright (497- 406 BC). Wrote more than 120 plays, but only seven are extant, including the Oedipus plays.

Sphinx – In *Oedipus the King*, a creature, part human and part animal, that terrorized the people of Thebes. If they could not solve her riddle, she killed them. Oedipus solved the riddle, defeated the Sphinx, and became king of Thebes.

Stymphalian Birds – They could shoot arrow-sharp feathers from their wings. Heracles killed them in the sixth of his 12 labors.

T-U

Tantalus – Founder of the House of Atreus. Murdered his son Pelops and offered his flesh to the gods to eat. They declined and restored Pelops' body. They subjected Tantalus to eternal punishment.

Tartarus – The underworld and one of the four primary deities. A deep abyss used as a dungeon of torment and suffering for the wicked and as the prison for the titans.

Telemachus – Son of Odysseus and Penelope. Stood with his father and fought the suitors.

GLOSSARY OF CHARACTERS

Theseus – Hero, protector and king of Athens. Son of King Aegeus as well as the god Poseidon. Known for slaying the Minotaur.

Thetis – Sea nymph mother of Achilles. Wife of Peleus. Fought for the Greeks.

Thisbe – See Pyramus and Thisbe.

Thucydides – Greek historian and general (460-400 BC). Wrote *The History of the Peloponnesian War* in 411 BC.

Thyestes – In the myth of the House of Atreus, brother of Atreus. Unknowingly ate his own two young sons that Atreus fed him. Sired another son, Aegisthus, to wreak vengeance.

Tiresias – In the Oedipus plays, blind prophet of Apollo at Thebes.

Turnus – In the *Aeneid*, prince of the Rutulians in Latium and Aeneas' enemy. Aeneas slaughtered him in battle.

Ulysses – See Odysseus.

Uranus – Sky. Son and mate of Gaia, the primordial couple, earth and sky. Castrated by Cronus and became the neutered dome of the sky.

V-W-X-Y-Z

Venus – See Aphrodite.

Virgil – Roman epic poet of the Augustan Age (70 - 19 BC). Wrote the *Aeneid*, but left it unfinished at his death (19 BC).

Vulcan – See Hephaestus.

Zeus – Among the ancient Greeks, Zeus was the sky and thunder god. He reigned as supreme ruler of the gods on Mount Olympus. He was the child of Cronus and Rhea and husband of Hera (and several others). Roman Jupiter or Jove.

ILLUSTRATIONS

COVER
Blind and Exiled: The Tragic Downfall of King Oedipus

BACK COVER
Pandora's Jar

INTRODUCTION
Map of Ancient Greece and Italy: First Millenium BC, *Page xiv*

CHAPTER I
Gaia, Mother Earth, *Page 6*

CHAPTER II
Zeus, Supreme Ruler of the Gods, *Page 10*
Athena, Goddess of Wisdom and Just War, *Page 31*

CHAPTER III
Prometheus, *Page 32*
Pandora's Jar, *Page 35*

CHAPTER IV
Heracles, Pan-Hellenic Greek Hero, *Page 40*
Theseus, Hero of Athens, Slays the Minotaur, *Page 47*

CHAPTER V
Helmet of an Ancient Greek Hero, *Page 52*
Brilliant Achilles, Greatest Greek Warrior, *Page 55*

CHAPTER VI
King Priam Begs Achilles for the Body of His Son Hector, *Page 73*

FROM SAVAGERY TO CIVILIZATION

CHAPTER VII
Odysseus and Calypso, *Page 76*

CHAPTER VIII
Homeric Code of Honor, *Page 88*
Xenia, *Page 91*

CHAPTER IX
Mask of Agamemnon, *Page 94*

CHAPTER X
Blind Oedipus, *Page 107*

CHAPTER XI
Romans Borrowed Greek Mythology, *Page 130*
The Three Graces, *Page 133*

CHAPTER XII
She-Wolf Rescued Romulus and Remus, *Page 136*

CHAPTER XIII
Aeneas Carrying Father Anchises from Falling Troy, *Page 138*

CHAPTER XIV
Pyramus and Thisbe, *Page 150*
Myth of Narcissus, *Page 153*

CHAPTER XV
Lightning-Wielding Zeus, *Page 160*
Athena Presides Over the Trial of Orestes, *Page 172*

ABOUT THE AUTHOR

VINCENT HANNITY

Vince Hannity's formal education includes a degree in English with minors in classical Greek and Latin, philosophy and education from Gonzaga University — earned more than 50 years before publication of this book. Since then, he and friends of like mind have continued an informal education studying the world's classic literature. Simultaneously, he pursued a rewarding business career with Boise Cascade Corporation, from which he is now retired. He served as Chair of the Idaho Humanities Council and the Idaho Commission on the Arts, and as member of other nonprofit boards. He and his wife, Janet, have four children and five grandchildren. The couple resides in Boise, Idaho.

COLOPHON

From Savagery to Civilization is designed in Classical style, with easy-to-read body copy and minimalist all-caps headlines. The headlines and sub-heads are set in COPPERPLATE GOTHIC, designed by typographic master Frederic Goudy and released by American Typefounders (ATF) in 1901. This Gothic font is not a true sans-serif typeface because it has very small serifs. It contains only capital letters and no italics, which made it desirable for formal printing such as invitations and proclamations. The body type is **Adobe Garamond Pro** designed by another type master, Robert Slimbach. Slimbach based this typeface after the 16th-century French engraver and printer Claude Garamond, whose typefaces were used for printing body text and books. Garamond's letter designs followed old letter punches by Fransisco Griffo in 1495, who used his old-style serif letters for Venetian printer Aldus Manutius. Adobe Systems released this classical typeface in 1989, with classic italics influenced by the designs of Garamond's assistant, Robert Granjon. Book design and typography by Meggan Laxalt Mackey, Studio M Publications & Design, Boise, Idaho. Illustrations by Meggan's daughter, Erin Ann Jensen, Vancouver, Washington.

www.ingramcontent.com/pod-product-compliance
Lightning Source LLC
Chambersburg PA
CBHW071356290426
44108CB00014B/1566